HEMINGWAY

A FAREWELL TO ARMS

NOTES

COLES EDITORIAL BOARD

Bound to stay open

Publisher's Note

Otabind (Ota-bind). This book has been bound using the patented Otabind process. You can open this book at any page, gently run your finger down the spine, and the pages will lie flat.

ABOUT COLES NOTES

COLES NOTES have been an indispensible aid to students on five continents since 1948.

COLES NOTES are available for a wide range of individual literary works. Clear, concise explanations and insights are provided along with interesting interpretations and evaluations.

Proper use of COLES NOTES will allow the student to pay greater attention to lectures and spend less time taking notes. This will result in a broader understanding of the work being studied and will free the student for increased participation in discussions.

COLES NOTES are an invaluable aid for review and exam preparation as well as an invitation to explore different interpretive paths.

COLES NOTES are written by experts in their fields. It should be noted that any literary judgement expressed herein is just that — the judgement of one school of thought. Interpretations that diverge from, or totally disagree with any criticism may be equally valid.

COLES NOTES are designed to supplement the text and are not intended as a substitute for reading the text itself. Use of the NOTES will serve not only to clarify the work being studied, but should enhance the reader's enjoyment of the topic.

ISBN 0-7740-3025-9

© COPYRIGHT 1996 AND PUBLISHED BY
COLES PUBLISHING COMPANY
TORONTO—CANADA
PRINTED IN CANADA

Manufactured by Webcom Limited
Cover finish: Webcom's Exclusive **Duracoat**

CONTENTS

Ernest Hemingway: Life and Works

Ernest Hemingway was not less literary than were other writers; it is simply that he approached literature as a method of direct action, a method of giving form and therefore meaning to an otherwise futile and violent universe.

Just as the matador in the bullfighting arena "makes love to death," and so asserts life by surrounding both with ritual, with courage and with will, so too does the writer act to create a dimension of truth and clarity from a nightmare vision of blind appetite or purposeless suffering. It is for good reason that Pedro, the matador in *The Sun Also Rises,* and Santiago, the fisherman in *The Old Man and the Sea,* are seen as men who are also artists—as individuals possessed of that quality of manhood essential for true living and true work. Neither Pedro nor Santiago retreats from the danger or cruelty of reality. They accept it with courage; they shape it through their power of will, achieving a triumph that states and redeems their morality.

If Hemingway made too much of literature as a kind of "fishing for the big one," if he saw the writer too exclusively as a sort of athlete-of-books, it is possible to say that he did so only because writing, for him, was neither a refuge nor a retreat from life, but rather its confrontation. The writer, the fisherman or the bullfighter is the solitary human being who faces the blank wall of time and uses his appropriate instrument—muleta, fishing line or typewriter— as a means of achieving the truth of form and dignity that alone give meaning to man's brief existence.

The Hemingway type of man was even more widely known than was the Hemingway type of book, and this in itself is an indication of how completely the restless teen-ager from Oak Park, Illinois had achieved a kind of glorification unparalleled in the history of American literature. So profoundly did the legend overshadow the man, and the man overshadow his books, that it often seemed as though the books were an incidental by-product of the life of Hemingway himself.

Perhaps the books were indeed a by-product, for no man had a greater zest for life, a greater appetite for action and travel, and a greater unwillingness to be known only as a literary figure. Passivity was something he avoided throughout his career, in his work as well as in his play (and for Hemingway, as for many artists, the two were closely related).

Certainly Ernest Hemingway considered life to be a kind of arena in which men used their courage, endurance and will as weapons. Certainly he considered life to be a perpetual struggle against a universe whose essential quality was one of irrational destruction, of violence without meaning. He also considered that literature was a ritual to be employed within the arena itself: a ritual of truth, precision and clarity in which a man could redeem his own inevitable defeat.

"He had destroyed his talent by not using it, by betrayals of himself . . . by laziness, sloth, and by snobbery, by pride," he says of the writer in "The Snows of Kilimanjaro," adding that "the thought of his own death obsessed him. . . ." This was a warning that Hemingway gave to himself many times in his life, with an intense honesty, characteristic of the man no less than that of his work. The thought of death was far more vital for Hemingway than a mere morbidity of attitude. Death, in a basic sense, is the ultimate honesty, the final fact that cannot be falsified or cheated. Faced with the fact of his own death, a man must see his own life clearly and truly. When the writer—softened and overprotected—forgets his own identity, and is no longer capable of his previous work, he affects the attitude that he no longer cares about that work.

Success and the Artist

Hemingway was aware of the danger of celebrity—the fact that success all too often destroys the very talent that it rewards. With the laurels of success come great pressures toward smugness and laziness, and—perhaps most important—a kind of fear of risking the possibility of failure. Let the writer become too comfortable in his success, he realized, and he—like the matador who plays it safe or the fisherman who stays too close to the shore—undergoes a kind of corruption for which no amount of displays, meant to fool the public, can compensate.

This would seem to be a peculiarly solemn self-reproach from a romantic adventurer. Perhaps it was not so peculiar after all, for Hemingway was, from the very beginning of his career, preoccupied with his craft, his art, his work. Even as a young man in Paris after World War I, Hemingway demonstrated a capacity for hard work, for artistic discipline, for voracious reading and calculated writing. Literature was never far from his mind, and he was occupied with far more than Parisian bar-hopping. His friends of those Parisian days make up a veritable "who's who" of literature: Ezra Pound,

F. Scott Fitzgerald, Ford Maddox Ford, Edmund Wilson, Gertrude Stein and many others—a long impressive list of novelists, poets and critics.

It was Gertrude Stein who once described Hemingway—despite his posture of impatience with bookish pursuits—as being a man of museums, but this description hardly fits the Sunday-supplement portrait of Hemingway the adventurer. In Paris, Hemingway was later to remember, he was trying to write and found that his greatest difficulty was to note what really happened in action, what the actual things were that produced the emotion that one experiences. He was trying to learn to write, commencing with the simplest things.

Hemingway's statement is a capsule definition of what he and other writers in the United States and abroad were trying to achieve during the post-World War I period: that is, an end to literary rhetoric, and a leaner, more objective, more concrete language that would not so much talk about emotion, as recreate it. The objective correlative of T. S. Eliot, for example, has much in common with Hemingway's cinematic prose—a detached, carefully accurate use of language as camera, so that the reader would not be told about a particular value of emotion, but would see the exact sequence of fact, object and action that created the emotion itself.

The Distrust of Rhetoric

Hemingway's distrust of literary rhetoric was shaped by his distrust of all abstractions that would substitute slogans for experience. The phony non-reality of verbalized Patriotism, Bravery, Love, Sacrifice or Nobility had been exposed, in the mass machinery of technological warfare, as a kind of sentimentality that falsified what it could not endure, and profited from what it sanctimoniously mourned. Hemingway, and other writers of his time, insisted that phrasemongering was the occupation of the politician or professional patriot; it was not the instrument of the writer. The literary artist would not use words for obscuring the reality of experience, but would use them as precisely and as economically as possible. Young writers had seen all the sacred abstractions and fine-sounding phrases of political, religious, literary and military leaders end in the dung heap of the World War I corpse factory; they demanded not more words, but fewer—words whose meaning would be clear and unmistakable, directed toward discovering experience and truth rather than avoiding them.

The fact remains, however, that not every experience has a meaning that is uniformly clear, nor a truth that is uniformly simple. Experience may evoke ambiguous implications, and truth may be complex. It is one thing for a writer to render complex experiences accurately, but quite another for him to insist that an experience must be uncomplicated in order to be valid. Hemingway's own refusal to deal with areas of complex being, rather than simple action, produces a certain limitation in his work. There is more to life than endurance, and there is more to dying than being killed. Perhaps one might also say that there is no more to growing old than the attempt to recapitulate the powers of youth—a fact that Hemingway seemed to find difficult to accept in his own lifetime, and that renders Santiago, in *The Old Man and the Sea,* in some ways pathetic rather than noble.

Limitations

That Hemingway's work has limitations is obvious enough, and it is unfortunate that efforts to elucidate these limitations have often aroused passions that have nothing to do with the work itself. Something of a Hemingway cult has arisen, which is encouraged by men who often seem more like cheerleaders than literary critics. Hemingway himself, of course, was partially responsible for this development. Haunted by fear of failure all his life—failure of art, failure of nerve, failure of other more intimate areas of existence—Hemingway could tolerate little criticism.

Too often he reacted to challenges with either denunciation or sulking, and questioned the motives, not to mention the manhood, of those who actually cared enough about his work to read it instead of merely praising it. His use of baseball-boxing-hunting jargon in the most absurd circumstances indicated that Hemingway had come to believe in his own colorful public image; untouched by self-perspective, the mannerisms had become the substance. "I trained hard and I beat Mr. de Maupassant," he boasted to Lillian Ross of the *New Yorker,* "I've fought two draws with Mr. Stendhal and I think I had an edge on the last one." Only Hemingway could have said it, and only Hemingway could have believed it.

It is always difficult, of course, to know when a writer's subject becomes an obsession, but Hemingway's insistence, and reinsistence, on virility and manhood do have their ludicrous aspects. One cannot escape the conclusion that his perpetual assertion had its basis in some murky feeling of anxiety. Certainly the Hemingway hero is too often either unaware of—or a refugee from—what is ultimately the most dangerous area of existence: the complexities of the human soul.

Action itself, after all, may be a narcotic—a way of making it unnecessary to confront any experience that cannot be handled as one handles a gun or fishing line. It is possible for a man to be so frightened of life that he feels compelled to kill something; to have so little feeling for life that his entire nature is directed toward endurance and the assertion of will; and to have so little understanding of life that he uses ritual as a substitute for reality rather than as a means of shaping it.

Throughout Hemingway's work there is a certain flight from all complexity. So often do Hemingway's heroes remind themselves not to think that we have no choice but to believe that they really mean it. It is true that Hemingway placed his heroes in situations in which thinking is not necessary—situations in which will and endurance become the primary human values. What such placing indicates, however, is the fact that Hemingway arranged his "stage sets" very carefully. He simply refused to deal with any aspect of real life—or even real struggle—that called for a wider arsenal of spiritual and intellectual weapons than those at the disposal of his protagonists or of Hemingway himself.

This reservation applies to his language as well. It may be true that, as Hemingway said, good prose is like an iceberg, with only a small part showing on the surface. But it is also true that icebergs must remain in chill and arctic waters—or they melt. If the hard surface of Hemingway's prose is in some ways admirable, in other ways it is the product of weakness rather than strength.

This is not to say that Hemingway's work is to be dismissed as insignificant. Indeed, it was precisely because Ernest Hemingway was an artist that he could turn his own failures, his own fears, into an art that is both significant and true. In order to understand what he did produce, it is necessary to have some idea of what he could not produce. Hemingway made the best possible use of his limitations, but we must recognize those limitations in order to appreciate the use to which he put them.

Basic Elements

Three elements in Hemingway's life shaped many of his attitudes, and indeed shaped much of his work: the fact that in World War I, he suffered a painful and terrible mortar wound, which made him conscious of the dread possibility of the loss of manhood; the fact that his father committed suicide; and the fact of his growing old—and the fears created by old age itself. Similar to Frederic Henry in *A Farewell to Arms,* Jake Barnes in *The Sun Also Rises,* and Santiago in *The Old Man and the Sea,* Hemingway was afflicted with the fear of letting go and the fear of thinking. The nightmare of chaos, of passivity—loss of will, loss of initiative, loss of the masculine role—was a terrible nightmare, and one to be avoided at all costs. That Hemingway evolved his own solutions to this nightmare, and based his art upon them, is something for which everyone interested in books and people must be thankful. We need not assume that the solutions were universal ones, nor need we shrink from examining the art itself.

World War I

Very few people—least of all the volunteers themselves—understood that World War I was to be the first great war of the machine, the first war in which mechanics were far more important than heroes, and the first war in which unprecedented masses of men slaughtered each other with little or none of the glory or tests of manhood that were supposed to be part of the military experience. Military leadership had not kept pace with technological advances, and few generals had any clear idea of how to control either the machines or the masses of men at their disposal. The result was a war in which individuals were reduced to helpless and hapless targets; a war in which the brave soldier and the cowardly soldier crawled about from one bloody hole to another and were likely to be killed—or not killed—quite by accident.

As a young boy in the Michigan north woods, deeply influenced by the examples and the philosophy of his father, Hemingway had learned to respect the strength and power of the individual creature— man or animal—alone with his own death. He had learned to respect courage and control, the right way of doing things, whether fishing for trout or killing game, and had gone to war at the age of nineteen expecting an exercise in manhood—an exercise in which the right way would be transferred to an orderly pattern of military form. What he encountered seemed to be a ridiculous joke, except that there was nothing funny about it.

The real political reason for the war, Hemingway and other young men of his generation were to discover, had little to do with the patriotic rhetoric and noble sentiments for which the newspapers and pulpits of America were responsible. Even as a personal test of

6

courage, the new kind of warfare was usually meaningless. Certainly it is true that for Ernest Hemingway the shock of mechanized and impersonal warfare was even greater than the shock of political corruption.

The tragic absurdity of the war was compounded by the fact that punitive courts-martial were too often a desperate resource of military leaders who had no idea of how to control the vast blood bath threatening to render obsolete all their neatly drawn maps and efficiently planned campaigns. The high commands remained tragically unaware of the social revolution that had led to the creation of civilian armies. Their attempts to apply methods of discipline appropriate to professional soldiers (who had traditionally been drawn from the lowest elements of the population), created chaos when used for the new armies of World War I.

The generals had very little notion of how to use their troops efficiently, and they tended to mistreat them. Soldiers were there to die; that was their function. When any plan miscarried, when any offensive or retreat failed to take place according to schedule (the Caporetto retreat in *A Farewell to Arms,* for example), those soldiers who survived were, by that very fact, suspect. Hence, Celine, the French novelist, remarks that the military administrations ''began to shoot troopers by squads so as to improve their morale.''

A New Generation

Having cast away the rose-colored spectacles of the older generation, young writers—including the young Ernest Hemingway—could look at the world around them with a fresh sense of truth. A world of moral and aesthetic values had been reduced to shambles in the conflagration of World War I. But fire cleanses as well as destroys and, after the war, young writers felt that they could—indeed, that they must—discover new values based not upon sentiment, but upon reality.

These values, of course, were widely divergent, whether in art, politics or literature. The young experimenters had one thing in common: they insisted that all values had to be based on truth. They wanted no more propaganda, no more inflated nonsense about home, mother and country. They were less interested in saving the world than in finding out what it is—or could be. And they rejected any solution that was not based on the facts. Since the truth about life was harsh, the solution—whatever it was—would have to cope with this harshness rather than ignore it. And if all solutions were false, if—given the nature of the world—they failed to work, the only answer would be to have no solution at all.

The Hemingway Code

In such case, a man would simply face up to reality with endurance, pride, courage and silence. Faced with futility, he would accept it. He would neither mouth sentimentalities nor invent lies to give meaning to a meaningless universe. He would endure. He would fashion a ritual of action that would exist by and for itself. He would create his own reality by imposing form upon chaos, and do this not only in work, but in talk and in play; there would be a code for men and women in the very words they used to each other, in the way they hunted, drank wine, made love, knew pleasure or suffered pain. In short, the individual—in the words of Jake Barnes of *The Sun Also Rises*—would act well rather than act badly, and in so doing would triumph over futility.

Such is the Hemingway code, which was to be a major element in all his books, and a sort of final resource for all his protagonists, from Jake Barnes in *The Sun Also Rises* (a war veteran rendered physically impotent by the absurd terrors of mechanized warfare), to Santiago in *The Old Man and the Sea* (an old fisherman rendered physically weak by age and isolation). Neither Jake nor Santiago, despite their respective weaknesses, suffers loss of manhood. This is a vital aspect of the Hemingway code, for manhood is a spiritual rather than a mere physical matter. Because they will their own endurance, pride and courage, Jake and Santiago emerge strong within their manhood—unlike those individuals who, despite an appearance of power, are less than men because of their lack of individual personalities.

While futility can be opposed by means of the code, it can never be wholly defeated. Realization of this fact is what separates the men from the boys in the world of Jake Barnes—and of Santiago-Hemingway as well. The good and brave go down into dust, into failure, no less inevitably than do the bad and cowardly; there is no magic formula that will deliver us from the *nada* (nothingness) that awaits us all. There is no ticket to a Palace of Perfect Bliss that will not prove to be in reality a ticket to nowhere at all. "All is vanity," says the voice of the Old Testament Ecclesiastes; and it was with deliberate calculation that Hemingway set the tone for his first literary success with a flyleaf quotation from this most profoundly sceptical of all Biblical books.

From the jumble of hopes for continued youth, and fears of age, however, one element emerges as perhaps the greatest fear of all—a fear that had been close to Hemingway from the crisis of his World War I experience; that is, the fear of passivity, the nightmare (a recurrent nightmare for Ernest Hemingway) in which the individual is deprived of his manhood by becoming an object rather than originator of action. Whether sitting on a park bench and waiting for death, or growing crotchety and senile in an easy chair, or whining and complaining in a hospital bed, the overriding fear is not loss of life ("it isn't hard to die," said Hemingway) but loss of initiative and will, the failure of manhood.

The problem, in short, was not how to avoid becoming an old man, but how to avoid becoming an old "woman." Whether Hemingway ever achieved a satisfactory solution to this dilemma is not for us to judge, although the circumstances of his death would indicate that he could not and would not abide a final weakening of those powers that were so important to the protagonists of his stories.

Early Years

Dr. Clarence E. Hemingway was a physician in Oak Park, Illinois. He was also an enthusiastic outdoorsman and a very domesticated—perhaps overdomesticated—husband to Grace Hall Hemingway, a religious and pious woman. The Hemingways had six children, and Clarence never failed in his duties as head of the family. He was a good provider, a sentimental husband and an affectionate father. In short, he was a solid and well-trained citizen who somehow felt it necessary to escape from the domestic hearth at every opportunity, using the Great Outdoors as a means of asserting whatever element of manhood or independence he felt was lacking in his family-directed (and perhaps woman-directed) home.

Young Ernest, the second of the Hemingway children (born July 21, 1899), was profoundly influenced by his father. Despite the efforts of Grace Hemingway to raise her son with a genteel education (she had ambitions to provide Ernest with a musical education), he followed the example of Clarence, and—very early indeed—made it clear that the only instruments he valued were fishing rods and guns: well cared for, religiously used and almost ritualistically maintained.

The typewriter too, however, was to become an instrument for the young Ernest Hemingway. Although he was never a very popular boy at school, he quickly demonstrated his ability to write accurately and well, and became the editor of his school paper. That he got the job was a tribute to his skill rather than his social success, for either through choice or nature (and perhaps a combination of both) he was never a member of the select social crowd. Indeed, his school experience was often lonely and not always pleasant, but it did provide one lesson that Hemingway was never to forget: life is a hard contest, which only the tough-minded are likely to survive.

Certain aspects of Hemingway's life at this time reflected his growing restlessness. He was determined, for example, to learn boxing, but was by no means a natural fighter; he achieved some mastery of boxing only at the cost of a broken nose and a serious eye injury. He actually ran away from home twice during his school years, and spent months "on the road" working at a variety of temporary and often laborious jobs.

The World War I Adventure

Akin to so many young men of the American Midwest, Ernest Hemingway was bored and waiting . . . waiting for some chance for adventure, for "winning his spurs" in a situation that would combine glory with danger. The European war seemed to offer just such a chance, and when America entered The Great Crusade in 1917, Hemingway promptly tried to enlist. His eye injury, however, kept him out of the service, and he had to settle for a job as cub reporter on the Kansas City *Star*. It became impossible for Hemingway to remain in Kansas City while thousands of other Americans were going off to earn their "red badges of courage" in battle and seek adventure. He volunteered to serve as an ambulance driver on the Italian front, and left America with his expectations; if he could not be a soldier, he would nevertheless taste the bitter glory of war.

It was a very brief taste indeed, and far more bitter than glorious. Only a few weeks after arriving in the combat zone, Ernest Hemingway was hit by a stray shell, receiving a serious wound that was to leave scars on his mind and spirit as well as on his body. It was, in many ways, an absurd wound, and one that had very little to do with soldiering at all. At the time he was hit he had been engaged in an activity that (under the circumstances) was rather ludicrous; he had been wounded while handing out chocolates to Italian soldiers.

According to Hemingway's own testimony, he was never to forget the impact of that experience. It was not so much the pain that he remembered as the manner in which the pain was inflicted—a helpless, passive receiving of a blow from an invisible "fist" of machinery and death. Indeed, it was the passivity rather than the pain that was to remain a nightmare for Hemingway throughout his career.

A situation in which a man could be flung on his back to receive, rather than give, a decisive blow threatened far more than life; it threatened manhood itself. In a very real sense Hemingway's life and his work were to be devoted to finding and exploring those areas of existence in which men could take the initiative from pain and death by surrounding it with form, with ritual and with willed endurance. There is, in short, an essential line of causation from Hemingway's traumatic experience during World War I to his subsequent preoccupation with the masculine role. In the fishing boat a man (Santiago in *The Old Man and the Sea*) could be alone with his pain, his own endurance and his own will—and the same is true of the bullfight arena or the hunt.

Post-World War I Days

During his post-World War I days in Paris, Hemingway was formulating the aesthetic basis of his work, while immersing himself deeply in the work of other writers—writers of the past as well as of the present. From Mark Twain to Henry James, from the English metaphysical poet, John Donne (who wrote in the seventeenth century), to the Russian writer, Turgenev (who wrote in the nineteenth), artists of a vast variety of epochs and cultures were grist for the young Hemingway's literary mill. The flyleaf quotations in his novels, which range from Donne to the Book of Ecclesiastes, have an oddly literary tone for a writer so often praised—and often caricatured in the praise itself—as a sort of Huckleberry Finn with a beard.

If his wound left vitally important scars on Hemingway's spirit, and if it brought his search for military glory to a violent and sudden end, it also seemed to sharpen his determination to live life as fully as he could, and to shape it according to his own talent and will. After returning to America, Hemingway became a writer for the Toronto *Star* and *Star Weekly,* and found himself involved with many literary people, the most important of whom was Sherwood Anderson. He was anxious to return to Europe, and after his marriage to Hadley Richardson in 1921, left the United States once again.

Hemingway as Journalist

This time he travelled widely throughout the continent, getting to know and love Spain, Switzerland, Austria and France. Meanwhile, he continued his work as a journalist, and enjoyed a rather sensational career in this respect. At the age of twenty-three he covered the Greek-Turkish war, and by the time he was twenty-five he had interviewed such world-famous figures as Lloyd George, Clemenceau and Mussolini.

After covering this war Hemingway went to Paris with an introduction from Sherwood Anderson and met Gertrude Stein, the *grande dame* of American literary expatriation. He was seriously trying to write at this time, but all was not going well with his marriage; Hadley was pregnant and wanted to return home. For Ernest Hemingway, however, Paris was home, and nothing—not even his wife and impending family—was more important than his literary work.

His stories had begun appearing in avant-garde and popular magazines (including *Atlantic Monthly),* and in 1923, he published *Three Stories and Ten Poems.* In 1924, *In Our Time*—a series of thirty-two fragments—was published in Paris. The collection of Nick Adams stories was published under the same title in the United States the following year, and *The Torrents of Spring* appeared in 1926. The literary career of Ernest Hemingway was underway at last, and nothing would be allowed to stop it.

Fame and Fortune

It was not until *The Sun Also Rises* appeared in late 1926, however, that Ernest Hemingway's name became a byword for millions of readers. With this novel the very phrase, "The Lost Generation," became a epithet for the disillusioned young people who had seen an entire world of ethical, moral and political values shattered in the chaotic butchery of World War I. "The Lost Generation," however (a phrase coined by Gertrude Stein in a remark to Hemingway himself), was in many ways a misleading label for the young writers and critics who came out of World War I convinced of the hypocrisy and shallowness of Western civilization. If such young people distrusted the sacred cows and sacred causes of their elders, it is also true that they did not sit back and sulk over their own disillusion. An end to an illusion, after all, is in itself not a harmful thing—and may actually be a stimulus rather than a depressant.

The Sun Also Rises made Hemingway the spokesman for the war generation. Its profound insistence upon the futility of abstract verbalisms, and its equally profound insistence that only a code of manners and action could combat this futility, captured the imagination of an age. Hemingway's personal life, however, was chaotic despite his literary success. A divorce ended his marriage to Hadley in 1927, and Hemingway—who never remained unmarried for long—wed Pauline Pfeiffer, an editor of *Vogue*, the same year. In 1928, Hemingway suffered an emotional shock rivalled only by the initial impact of the war: the death of his father, by a self-inflicted gunshot wound, under circumstances that were to be tragically repeated in the death of Ernest Hemingway himself.

Late in 1928, Hemingway left Europe and took up residence at Key West, Florida, where Patrick Hemingway was born in 1929 and Gregory in 1932. His second major work, *A Farewell to Arms*, had appeared in 1929. The book was an immediate critical and financial success, earning the applause of readers everywhere and selling 80,000 copies in four months.

Hemingway as "Papa"

There was no doubt that Hemingway enjoyed his fame and fortune; he was far too fond of the good things of life ever to be reluctant about accepting the rewards of literary celebrity. The man who liked to call himself "Papa" and "The Champ" was hardly a paragon of personal modesty, and his exploits in Third Avenue bars no less than on African safaris were the delight of Sunday-supplement writers. So determinedly did Hemingway pursue his own colorful image, that he sometimes seemed to parody himself. The profile written by Lillian Ross for the *New Yorker* magazine in 1952 is a delightful delineation of the author's personal absurdities and of his charm.

It was not enough, however, for Ernest Hemingway to be a celebrity. He was a writer, and the job of the writer is to write. Behind all the public clowning and Sunday-supplement posturing, apart from his various roles as soldier of fortune or grizzled old warrior, Hemingway remained true to the part of his being that was neither public nor posture: the part of himself that, alone in the arena, had to carve out a ritual of meaning from blankness.

Living in Key West after the appearance of *A Farewell to Arms*, and rapidly outgrowing his physical youth, Hemingway began moving from the role of "Champ" to the role of "Papa"—a posture (and a name) he was to enjoy throughout the remainder of his career. Possessed of great financial security as a result of his two best-selling novels, the acknowledged leader of an entire literary generation, the father of three sons (John Hemingway was the son of his first marriage); Ernest Hemingway was free to write, to fish, to hunt and to travel—a freedom that he utilized with characteristic enthusiasm. In 1932, *Death in the Afternoon* appeared, and in 1933, *Winner Take Nothing* was published. During 1933, Hemingway also published the first of thirty-one articles and stories that were to appear in *Esquire* regularly for the next six years.

Hemingway and the Spanish Civil War

Hemingway, of course, was not one to stay in one place for long—not even in his lovely Key West home. He travelled extensively, especially in Africa, and one result of his journeying was *The Green Hills of Africa,* which appeared in 1935. With the outbreak of the Spanish Civil War in 1936, Hemingway entered the arena of international politics. How much of Hemingway's motivations were actually ideological or political is open to speculation, but one thing is certain: the war in Spain was a political as well as military battleground. Hemingway had to choose his side in ideological terms if he was to justify his interest in this war.

He devoted himself to the cause of the Loyalists, or anti-Fascists and, in 1937, served in Spain as a correspondent for the North American Newspaper Alliance—service that was to solidify his hatred of the Fascist war machine, but that also resulted in considerable disillusion with the cause of the Loyalists as well. The war had revealed itself to be not simply a matter of virtue against vice, nor of saving the Spanish people and land that Hemingway loved so deeply, but rather had shown itself to be a complex and murky swamp of political ambiguities, of intellectual cross purposes, of propaganda and cruelty and expediency that too often appeared unrelated to any noble cause whatsover.

Meanwhile, Hemingway was making an attempt to assert social rather than individual value and responsibilities. In 1937, with *To Have and Have Not* (three related stories, two of which had been published separately), Hemingway took the position that a man cannot stand alone—that he must have a cause beyond himself for which he can fight and die. Once again it can be debated whether Hemingway was truly interested in any cause per se, or whether his imagination responded to "a cause" only as a means to legitimize what had always been his chief theme and preoccupation, the fighting and the dying itself.

Hemingway and World War II

After completing *For Whom the Bell Tolls,* Hemingway once again faced a crisis in his personal life and, in 1940, he and Pauline first separated and then were divorced. He promptly married the writer, Martha Gelhorn and, in 1940, began new travels with his new wife. After visiting China, they settled in Cuba. When World War II erupted, Hemingway leaped into the fray in his own manner. After editing *Men at War* in 1942, he served as a war correspondent, accompanying American troops as they pushed the German forces back across western Europe.

Hemingway, of course, took to his new war with enthusiasm. Known as "Papa" to respectful troops, and a celebrity everywhere, he helped "liberate" the Ritz Hotel in Paris, actually posting a guard at the entrance with a notice: "Papa took good hotel. Plenty stuff in cellar." It was, however, Hemingway's last war adventure. The increasing complexity of ideological warfare and police actions against communism eliminated war itself as an aesthetic resource for Hemingway. Not until he left war and politics altogether, and took to Santiago's small boat on the open sea, did Hemingway produce another major work of fiction.

The preoccupation of Hemingway with individual courage, will and endurance could not help but be seriously threatened in a time of political upheaval, a time that more than ever before represented the triumph of machines over men. World War II, certainly, was a difficult subject for Hemingway to shape into art—especially since so much of his art had been based upon the need for self-contained action, ritualized form, precision of motion (and emotion) and— perhaps most important—the insistence on the absolute necessity of personal initiative as a prerequisite of manhood.

The war, for one thing, had been a gigantic operation in which the politician became more important than the soldier, and the mechanic became far more important than both.

As for the post-World War II era of Cold War and continuing crisis—there was simply nothing in it for Hemingway to use. This aspect of Hemingway's work was clarified by Nemi D'Agostino in his article, "The Later Hemingway" (*Hemingway: A Collection of Critical Essays,* ed. Robert P. Weeks, Prentice-Hall, 1962).

Old Age as Nightmare

For Ernest Hemingway, far more than for most men, the specter of age was a terrible specter indeed; the very virtues upon which he had based his life and his art were virtues of the young. Even in his later years, Hemingway was delightfully boyish (or regrettably so, depending on one's point of view); the problem of age was never far from his mind nor, for that matter, from his conversation—in this connection, Lillian Ross' *New Yorker* piece on Hemingway (May 31, 1950) is of particular interest. "As you get older," said Hemingway, "it is harder to have heroes, but it is sort of necessary."

The problem, of course, is to decide what sort of heroism is possible as a man does get older, and in this respect, Hemingway, in 1950, was still looking backward rather than forward, so that for him (as for Robert Cantwell in *Across the River and Into the Trees*) old age itself was still simply a matter of holding onto youthful appetites and youthful abilities as long as he could. "What I want to be when I am old is a wise old man who won't bore," he remarked to Miss Ross:

> I'd like to see all the new fighters, horses, ballets, bike-riders, dames, bullfighters, airplanes, sons of bitches, café characters, big international whores, restaurants, years of wine, newsreels, and never have to write a line about any of it. . . . Would like to make good love until I was eighty-five.

Throughout the interview there is a note of buoyancy combined with uncertainty, of readiness for death juxtaposed with fear of aging, of awareness of the inevitable combined with almost wistful assertion of youthful power, and—finally—a kind of subdued self-perspective in which Hemingway seems to be doubting his own verbal posture. All these clashing elements were intrinsic in Hemingway's own position, as they were in the position of his protagonist in *Across the River and Into the Trees*.

In the last decade or so of his life, Hemingway was searching for a posture that would enable him to cope with the fact of his own age; and in a basic sense, *Across the River and Into the Trees* reflected the urgency of just such a search. Hemingway's temporary but vivid solution was a change of personal role; he would dramatize what he could not avoid. "Because of his own absolute youthfulness," prophetically remarked one of his close friends, "he regards old-growing as an utter and complete tragedy . . . and he is not going to degrade himself by maturing or anything of that sort. All the same, since he has a sense of costume, he will emphasize his decline in all its hopelessness by sprouting a white beard and generally acting the part of *senex*. We are going to get a lot of this inverted youth from him henceforth.'' (Quoted by Carlos Baker, *Hemingway and His Critics*, New York, 1961, p. 9.)

If the early Hemingway had been an almost legendary figure of youthful and virile adventure, the older Hemingway would take up the role of Grand Old Man, the battle-scarred veteran, the aging but still indomitable combatant. Hemingway ''the Champ'' would become ''Papa'' Hemingway—citizen of the world, still rough-edged and manfully poetic, but mellowed by experience and years, and come to full bloom as a connoisseur of life, bullfighters, women, fishing and war.

Hemingway had by no means retired from active working and living. Divorced from Martha in 1944, he immediately married Mary Walsh, a *Time Magazine* correspondent. *Across the River and Into the Trees* appeared, and met with much critical disapproval. Hemingway, it seemed clear, had entered too completely into the role of Grand Old Man of American Literature; his style had become mannered, and his aging protagonist seemed to lack the intellectual equipment for the heavy burden of introspection with which Hemingway loaded his narrative.

The ''Old Man'' and the Nobel Prize

This negative critical response infuriated Hemingway. *The Old Man and the Sea,* which appeared in 1952, was seen by some readers as an attempt on the critical ''sharks'' themselves. One might note that there was some justification for Hemingway's resentment. Any writer with his force of personality must expect to make literary enemies, and Hemingway had created perhaps more than his share of personal resentment. Too many critics, at any rate, had seemed to get a kind of satisfaction from the failure of *Across the River and Into the Trees,* and Hemingway—as usual—was not very hesitant about expressing his scorn for gentlemen who seemed so willing to serve as mourners at the burial of a literary career still very much alive.

After the publication of *The Old Man and the Sea,* Hemingway travelled once again and, in 1954, he narrowly escaped death in an airplane crash. This event occurred the same year he received the

Nobel Prize for literature. Hemingway's health was failing. After a period of illness, he met his death as the victim of a "self-inflicted gunshot wound" in 1961, at Ketchum, Idaho, in the rugged country he loved so well. He had been working until the end, leaving many unpublished manuscripts in the care of Mary; and in 1963 there appeared his posthumous—and best-selling—memoir of Paris in the twenties: *A Moveable Feast*.

Other manuscripts remain unpublished, and the world has not yet heard the last from Ernest Hemingway, who—whether or not "the Champ" of American Literature—was a major contender in our own or any other language.

Introduction to *A Farewell to Arms*

There is nothing particularly complicated about *A Farewell to Arms*. It would appear to be simply the story of two people who meet in an unlikely place and fall in love. But there is a war going on and their lives are altered by it.

In a sense, the plot conforms to the classic formula: boy meets girl, boy loses girl, boy gets girl back. But Hemingway alters the last chapter.

As in almost every great novel, there are elements of the autobiographical in this one. Like the hero of the novel, Hemingway was himself a Red Cross ambulance driver on the Italian front in World War I. He was also severely wounded in the legs by mortar fragments and heavy machine-gun fire. But all this was after (not before, as in the novel) the Italians' disastrous retreat from Caporetto, so we can only presume that he wrote about the retreat from what he had heard. Also, the love story is evidently of Hemingway's invention. But he knows the locale and the people and, by the credo that states that a writer should write only about what he knows, Hemingway is true to his craft.

This is not a pleasant story. In some of the descriptions of war, Hemingway's narrative is every bit as gruesome as the horrific tales that were written about World War II. There is one difference, however; he writes far better. And, at the same time, Hemingway's is a shining and beautiful story of the love of two people who need each other in a period of upheaval.

"Ernest Hemingway was already regarded [before the publication of *A Farewell to Arms* in 1929], by a limited literary public, as a writer of extraordinary freshness and power, as one of the makers, indeed, of a new American fiction," says Robert Penn Warren. "*A Farewell to Arms* more than justified the early enthusiasm of the connoisseurs for Hemingway and extended this reputation from them to the public at large. Its great importance was at once acknowledged, and its great importance has survived through the changing fashions and interests of twenty years."

That was written in 1949, as an introduction to yet another edition of this novel. It is still regarded as true today. Other authors of note have written about World War I, but *A Farewell to Arms* remains to this day the most remembered book in English about that epoch.

A Farewell to Arms is near the high-water mark of Hemingway's work. Few other novels were able to convey so movingly the sterility of motivation and the bitterness that characterized many participants in World War I. The love affair between Lieutenant Henry and Catherine Barkley, taking place in a tragic counterpoint to growing weariness, detachment, cynicism and retreat suggested both the complexity of living and the irrevocability of doom. *A Farewell to Arms*, for all the darkness of its perceptions, did not cheapen the theme of death as did some of Hemingway's later work, where death is evoked with a hunter's boasting, or demeaned through the overtones of a simplistic adolescence.

This is one of the all-time great stories of war and love. *Farewell* is a great deal more than a war story. It is a great love story, a modern *Romeo and Juliet* in its intensity and tragedy. But the love story could not have taken place without the background of war, and therein lies its tragedy and its beauty.

All of Hemingway's novels are tragedies. Indeed, some critics have accused him of being obsessed with death, while others maintain that he is simply depicting the essential reality of life. In any case, one does not read Hemingway expecting a happy ending. There is a doom that hangs over this novel from the very first chapter, yet Hemingway's skilful construction does allow the immediate appearance of stark tragedy; he provides a sort of roller coaster, happy-sad, life-death tempo that brings us to the last chapter uplifted, only to be cast down into the depths of sadness.

The critic, Carlos Baker, says of this novel:

Neither in *Romeo and Juliet* nor in *A Farewell to Arms* is the catastrophe a direct and logical result of the immoral social situation. Catherine's bodily structure, which precludes a normal delivery for her baby, is an unfortunate biological accident. The death of Shakespeare's lovers is also precipitated by an accident—the detention of the message-bearing friar. The student of esthetics, recognizing another kind of logic in art than that of mathematical cause-and-effect, may however conclude that Catherine's death, like that of Juliet, shows a kind of artistic inevitability. Except by a large indirection, the war does not kill Catherine any more than the Veronese feud kills Juliet. But in the emotional experience of the novel, Catherine's dying is directly associated and interwoven with the whole tragic pattern of fatigue and suffering, loneliness, defeat and doom, of which the war is itself the broad and social manifestation. And one might make a similar argument about *Romeo and Juliet*.

Stylistically, the novel exists on the level of those wonderful stories that declared the author's uniqueness. The *49 Stories* contain less violence and more sympathetic examinations of human relationships than the conventional view of Hemingway's reputation would suggest. The retreat of the Italian forces has been described as Hemingway's best narrative passage. The dialogue between Henry and Catherine is filled with the sensations of those unspoken, but recognizable, overtones shared by lovers in private. The stripping away of all superfluous matter, the simplified sentence structure learned in the Paris years, the heightened awareness of natural forces— these are some of the aspects of *A Farewell to Arms* that will retain for the novel a lasting place in the history of American fiction. It will remain safe, most likely, from the assaults that time makes upon those works whose prominence rests too greatly upon transitory fashions. In this book, Hemingway largely succeeded in his search for the appearance of things as he felt them to really be. The grace of a poet and the disciplined craftsmanship of a novelist combined to produce a novel that is far more than the picture of a small episode in World War I.

Plot Summary

Lieutenant Frederic Henry is a young American volunteer who is serving as an ambulance driver in the Italian army during World War I. A major offensive is soon to begin and Henry has just returned to the front from leave. He learns from his room-mate, Rinaldi, that a group of English nurses had arrived during his absence. Furthermore, Rinaldi claims to have fallen in love with one of the newcomers—Catherine Barkley—and, the next day, he introduces Henry to her.

Between ambulance trips to evacuation posts at the front, Henry calls on Miss Barkley frequently. He likes the frank, young English girl in a casual sort of way, but he is not in love with her. Before he leaves for the front she gives him a St. Anthony medal to wear during the battle.

At the front, as Henry and some Italian ambulance drivers are eating in a dugout, an Austrian mortar shell explodes over them. Henry, badly wounded in the legs, is taken to a field hospital. Later, he is moved to a hospital in Milan.

Before the doctor is able to see Henry in Milan, the nurses forbid him to drink wine, but he bribes a porter to bring him a supply, which he keeps hidden behind his bed. Catherine Barkley comes to the hospital and Henry knows that he is in love with her. The doctors tell Henry that he will have to lie in bed for six months before they can operate on his knee. Henry insists on seeing another doctor, who tells him that the operation can be performed the next day. Meanwhile, Catherine manages to be with Henry constantly.

After his operation, Henry convalesces in Milan while Catherine Barkley sees to his needs. Together they dine in out-of-the-way restaurants and they ride about the countryside in a carriage. Henry is restless and lonely at night, so Catherine often comes to his hospital room.

Summer passes into autumn. Henry's wound has healed and he is due to take convalescent leave in October. He and Catherine plan to spend the leave together, but he comes down with jaundice before he can leave the hospital. The head nurse accuses him of bringing on the jaundice by drink, in order to avoid being sent back to the front.

Before he leaves for the front, Henry and Catherine stay together in a hotel room. She has already disclosed to him that she is pregnant.

Henry returns to the front with orders to load his three ambulances with hospital equipment and go south into the Po valley. Morale is at a low ebb. Rinaldi admires the surgery that has been done on Henry's knee and observes that Henry has begun to act like a married man. War weariness has spread throughout the army. At the front, the Italians have learned that German divisions are reinforcing the Austrians, and, fearing for their lives, they begin their terrible retreat from Caporetto. Henry drives one of the ambulances loaded with hospital supplies. During the retreat south, the ambulance is held up several times by wagons, guns and trucks, which extend in stalled lines for miles. Henry picks up two straggling Italian sergeants. During the night, the retreat is halted for hours by the rain.

At daybreak, Henry cuts out of the long line and drives across country in an attempt to reach Udine by side roads. The ambulance gets bogged down in a muddy side road. The sergeants decide to leave, but Henry asks them to help dislodge the car from the mud. They refuse and run. Henry shoots and wounds one of them, but the other escapes across the fields. An Italian ambulance corpsman with Henry shoots the wounded sergeant through the back of the head.

Henry and his three comrades set out on foot for Udine. On a bridge, Henry sees a German staff car and German bicycle troops crossing another bridge over the same stream. Within sight of Udine, one of Henry's men is killed by a nervous Italian sniper. The others hide in a barn until it seems safe to circle around Udine and join the mainstream of the retreat toward the Tagliamento River.

By this time, the Italian army is nothing but a frantic mob. Soldiers are throwing down their arms and officers are cutting the badges of rank from their sleeves. At the end of a long wooden bridge across the Tagliamento, military carabinieri are seizing all officers, giving them drumhead trials and executing them by the river bank. Henry is detained, but in the dark of night he breaks free, plunges into the river and escapes on a log. He crosses the Venetian plain on foot, then jumps aboard a freight train and rides to Milan, where he goes to the hospital in which he had been a patient. There he learns that Catherine has gone to Stresa.

With the events surrounding the retreat from Caporetto, Henry had made his farewell to arms. He borrows civilian clothes from an American friend in Milan and goes by train to Stresa, where he meets Catherine. The bartender of the hotel in which Henry is staying warns Henry that the authorities are planning to arrest him for desertion the next morning. He offers his boat to Henry and Catherine so they can escape to Switzerland. Henry accepts and, after rowing all night, his hands are so raw that he is barely able to touch the oars. Over his protests Catherine takes a turn at the rowing.

They reach Switzerland safely but are arrested. Henry tells the police that he is a sportsman who enjoys rowing and that he has come to Switzerland for the winter sports. The valid passports and the ample funds that Henry and Catherine possess save them from serious trouble with the authorities.

During the rest of the fall and the winter, the couple stay at an inn outside Montreux. They discuss marriage, but Catherine will not be married while she is pregnant. They hike, read and optimistically talk about what they will do together after the war.

When the time for Catherine's confinement approaches, she and Henry go to Lausanne to be near a hospital. They plan to return to Montreux in the spring. At the hospital, Catherine's pains prompt the doctor to use an anesthetic on her. After hours of suffering, she gives birth to a stillborn child. The nurse sends Henry out to get something to eat. When he returns to the hospital, he learns that Catherine has had a hemorrhage. He goes into the room and stays with her until she dies. There is nothing he can do, no one he can talk to, no place he can go. Catherine is dead. He leaves the hospital and walks back to his hotel in the dark. It is raining.

Characters in the Novel

FREDERIC HENRY: Young American who is a second lieutenant in the Italian army.

THE CAPTAIN: An Italian army captain who delights in badgering the priest in Henry's unit.

THE PRIEST: The good man from the mountains; the chaplain in Henry's outfit.

THE MAJOR: The quiet man who is in charge of Henry's outfit.

RINALDI: Henry's room-mate, an Italian surgeon; a woman-chaser.

CATHERINE BARKLEY: The female protagonist; English volunteer nurse.

HELEN FERGUSON: Scottish nurse; good friend of Catherine.

PASSINI, MANERA, GAVUZZI, GORDINI: Henry's ambulance drivers; all mechanics from northern Italy and all socialists or communists.

MRS. WALKER: American nurse at the hospital in Milan.

MISS GAGE: Another American nurse at the Milan hospital; friendly with Henry and Catherine.

MISS VAN CAMPEN: Superintendent of nurses at the American hospital in Milan; hostile to Henry.

DR. VALENTINI: Italian surgeon who operates on Henry for removal of shrapnel from his legs.

MEYERS: A mysterious old American who lives in Milan.

ETTORE MORETTI: An Italian from San Francisco; a hero in the war.

RALPH SIMMONS: American studying singing in Italy.

BONELLO, PIANI, AYMO: Ambulance drivers.

BARMAN: The bartender at the hotel in Stresa who helps Henry and Catherine to escape to Switzerland.

COUNT GREFFI: Patriarch who plays billiards with Henry in Stresa.

GUTTINGENS: Keepers of the inn where Henry and Catherine stay in Switzerland.

THE DOCTOR: The Swiss doctor who is in attendance when Catherine dies.

Chapter Summaries and Commentaries

BOOK I · CHAPTER 1

Summary
In the first chapter the scene is set. The period is World War I (probably 1916, though this is not explained) and the place is the Italo-Austrian front in the Alps, along what is now the Austrian and Yugoslav border of Italy, at that time a part of the Austro-Hungarian Empire. The story is told in the first person by an American volunteer in the Italian ambulance corps, Frederic Henry. (We only learn of this in later chapters.) He describes the mountains, the plains, the troops passing by and the fighting in the mountains, which is not going well. He ends the chapter by remarking that, at the start of winter, the rains started and there was an epidemic of cholera in the army.

Commentary
The first chapter does little more than set the scene, but it is a fine example of Hemingway's tight, disciplined style. Not a word is wasted, and when we have read the 500 or so words, we have been given a description of a war front that is vivid and realistic.

The description of the passing troops sets the mood for a book that does not glamorize war. The troops marching in the mud, the officers going by in their cars splashing mud, and the almost daily inspections by the king all add up to a campaign that is going "very badly," as Hemingway tells us. The chapter ends with an almost casual reference to the fact that when winter came there was an epidemic of cholera in the army, but "only seven thousand died." All of this sets the scene for the tragic happenings to come.

So far, we do not know who is telling the story. The only indication that it is being told in the first person is the use of "we" on several occasions. Later, we will learn that the narrator is Frederic Henry, a second lieutenant in the Italian Army, an American volunteer in the ambulance corps.

Some critics have said that Hemingway uses this chapter to establish the symbolism of mountain and plain for good and evil and of rain for tragedy. It is possibly a little early for such interpretations. However, the significance of physical symbols will become evident in later chapters.

To put the scene in its historical context, it should be noted that Italy, as an ally of Britain and France and Imperial Russia, was engaging the forces of the Austro-Hungarian Empire. The front ran from the Swiss border in the Otztaler Alps across the Austrian border in the Carnic Alps to the Julian Alps along the Yugoslav frontier, and down into the plains around Trieste. It was Italy's job to keep the Austro-Hungarian forces occupied so that they could not actively help Germany on the Western and Eastern fronts. Italy succeeded in doing this, but the collapse of Russia and sufferings at home brought on revolutionary riots in Turin in 1917 and affected the morale of the troops at the front. This is the period of which Hemingway writes. In the end, the Italians were victorious, but at a fearful cost. They had lost 600,000 soldiers and had over one million wounded, of whom some 220,000 were permanently maimed.

This is the locale and the background of the novel. It will help to keep in mind that the fighting went on in the mountains as well as in the plains and that Italy has a common border with Switzerland. Switzerland was neutral in World War I, just as she has been neutral in all wars for hundreds of years. This has a bearing on the story.

Notes

Camion: A truck used to carry cannons.

King: The reference is to King Victor Emmanuel III (1869-1947), who was a very small man. He came to the throne in 1900 and abdicated in 1945.

Udine: A city in Venezia Euganea, northeast Italy, 61 miles from Venice. It was a military base for operations against Austria.

Austria-Hungary: The former Austro-Hungarian Empire included Austria, Hungary, Czechoslovakia, Bucovina and Transylvania in Romania, the northwest half of Yugoslavia, Galicia in Poland, Venezia Guilia and Venezia Tridentina in Italy. It collapsed after World War I.

CHAPTER 2

Summary

The story line is not advanced in this chapter, but we learn that it is now the next year and that the fighting is going well. The narrator is staying in Gorizia, where his outfit is located. We meet some of the narrator's fellow officers, including the chaplain, who is the butt of many of the officers' jokes. We also learn that there are two bawdy houses (brothels) in the town, one for officers and the other for enlisted men. The captain jokingly accuses the priest of frequenting them and the priest is embarrassed. We learn that the narrator is preparing to go on leave, and the officers suggest various places he should visit.

Commentary

Hemingway has now moved into the second phase of his story. He is setting the physical scene more firmly and also introducing the theme of the book. Stated very simply, it is love against hate, good against evil. We have not entered the mainstream of the story by any means yet, but the cast of characters is being introduced and, more importantly, the mood is being set.

Gorizia, the scene of this chapter, is a town behind the lines that once belonged to the Austrians. It is, we gather, the headquarters of Frederic Henry's detachment, although we are still not told its duties. The existence of two brothels, one for officers and one for the other men, should not surprise Americans: it was a common practice in most armies.

The scene in the mess, while it may appear to be nothing more than an idle soldier's chaffing of a young priest, is most significant. Note that Henry takes no part in the kidding. This is, in many ways, a religious book and here is the first indication we get of the forces of good being attacked by the forces of evil. Good, symbolized by the priest, is attacked by evil, symbolized by the captain.

Note the additional symbolism that critics such as Carlos Baker (*Hemingway, The Writer as Artist,* Princeton University Press, 1952) and Robert Penn Warren dwell on at some length. This is what Baker calls the Mountain and the Plain. The priest from the mountain country of Abruzzi is the symbol of the mountain—the good—while the captain from the lowlands is the symbol of the plain—the bad. This will come out again and again later, but it is important to keep it in mind here as it will aid you in understanding how Hemingway has planned the story.

Notes

Gorizia: A strategic, small city in northeastern Italy, captured by the Italians from the Austrians in 1916. It is close to the present Yugoslav border.

Carso: A mountain plateau north of Trieste and east of the Isonzo River. The greater part of it is in Yugoslavia.

Asti: A province in northwest Italy. The reference here is to Asti Spumante, a famous sparkling (bubbly) wine.

Pidgin Italian: The captain's dialogue should make it plain what is meant by this, but as Hemingway says, it was "for my doubtful benefit."

Franz Joseph: The Emperor Franz Joseph, the last Hapsburg ruler of the Austro-Hungarian Empire.

"Black Pig": Apparently a reference to an antireligious book.

Free Masons: The oldest and most powerful secret society in the world. The Roman Catholic Church opposes it. For a fuller explanation consult any encyclopedia.

Abruzzi: A town in the Apennine Mountains.

Soto-Tenente, etc.: The ranks should be self-explanatory. *Tenente* is lieutenant and *soto* means "under," or what we call a second lieutenant. There is no such rank as *soto-colonello*.

Caruso: Enrico Caruso, the greatest operatic tenor of his day.

CHAPTER 3

Summary

Lieutenant Henry returns to Gorizia after his leave to find that little has changed. There are more guns around and some new hospitals, one staffed by the British. He is greeted by his room-mate, Rinaldi, the surgeon, who asks him if he has had a good time. Rinaldi wants details of Henry's amorous adventures and, in turn, tells him that the town now has beautiful girls, including the one he is in love with, Miss Barkley. That night at the mess Henry meets the priest again. The priest is unhappy that Henry did not visit Abruzzi. The captain is still baiting the priest, but the major tells him to leave the priest alone.

Commentary

In this chapter we are introduced to Rinaldi, Henry's room-mate. Rinaldi is an exuberant Italian, emotional and fiery. He has no particular bearing on the story, but does help in setting a mood.

Rinaldi speaks of the beautiful English girls and of a certain Miss Barkley "I am now in love with." Rinaldi is, of course, always in love with someone, and Henry's casual acceptance of the statement is indicative of how much stock he puts in Rinaldi's romantic attachments. But the introduction of both characters has been made and it will be significant later. This is a playwright's device, to introduce a character before actually bringing the person on stage, and Hemingway is performing the function of playwright at this point.

The symbolism of mountain and plain brought out in the last chapter is again displayed here in the talk Henry has with the priest. Note how he says he had been to no place where it was clean, but to places in the plains where he had caroused, "to the smoke in cafes. . . ." The contrast between the places he had been to and the "clean and cold" places described by the priest is brought out in a typical Hemingway paragraph in which Henry tries to explain to the priest why he did not go to Abruzzi. The plains are where evil is, the mountains are where there are many things, including "good hunting."

Note, too, how Hemingway shows us that Henry is apparently the only officer who is friendly with the priest. The other officers, being Italian, are presumably Roman Catholics, and Henry is not, as will be shown later, yet he is the only one of the group who shows respect for the man of religion. Hemingway is gradually revealing that, while Henry will behave like many other soldiers in time of war, he also has an interest in spiritual things even though they may not be formalized in the name of religion. Carnal love is at one end of the scale and pure love at the other.

Notes

Schutzen Stock: Schutzen, in this context, means "to shoot." The gun is apparently a fine hunting rifle.

Ciaou: A familiar Italian greeting; a sort of American "hi."

Milano, Firenze, Roma, Napoli: The Italian names for Milan, Florence, Rome, Naples.

Lira: The Italian lira, at this time was worth about ⅕ of an American dollar.

Strega: An Italian liqueur.

CHAPTER 4

Summary

Lieutenant Henry inspects his ambulance unit in the morning and discovers that everything is fine. As he says, the whole thing seemed to run better while he was away. In the evening, he goes with Rinaldi to call on the English nurses, Miss Barkley and Miss Ferguson. Henry talks with Miss Barkley and learns that the man she was engaged to had been killed in France the year before. She dwells at some length on this. On the way home, Rinaldi remarks that Miss Barkley apparently prefers Henry to himself.

Commentary

The first part of the chapter is uneventful although it does show in some slight degree that Henry is on good terms with the men in his unit. The real significance of the chapter, however, is in the meeting with Miss Barkley, the English nurse.

From the moment that Henry and Rinaldi arrive at the hospital, the story is carried almost entirely in dialogue. We learn only that Miss Barkley is "quite tall," a blonde with "tawny skin and gray eyes," and that Henry thinks she is very beautiful. Hemingway never paints long word-pictures of his characters and, aside from references such as these, the reader is left to draw his own imagination-portrait of the individual. For instance, while Rinaldi is never described, we gather that he is dark, good looking and a dandy.

At their first meeting, Miss Barkley talks of her young fiancé who was killed in the battle at Somme. At one point, she asks Henry if he has ever loved anyone, and Henry says he has not. This should be borne in mind, just as Miss Barkley's remark should be, that he— meaning her late fiancé—"could have had anything he wanted." We have, at this moment, a man who admits to never having loved and a woman who does not seem sure whether she has or not. It should be kept in mind, too, that this is a story of people involved in a war and, in wartime, love, life and death are all going at a much faster pace than normally.

At this point, we gather that Henry is interested in Miss Barkley. She is beautiful and Henry is "on the make." This fits in with his character as we have learned about it so far from his visits to the brothel and his adventures during his leave.

While it is brought out only in passing, the British attitude about Italians—or non-British "foreigners" in general—will have a bearing on the future course of the story. "What an odd thing—to be in the Italian army," Miss Barkley says. This will come out again later. The point is, that the British somehow thought of the Italian front as a "picturesque"—quite different from the French front, which was where a war was really being fought. Why an Anglo-Saxon American should be in the Italian army is something that Miss Barkley cannot understand.

Notes

On Permission: On leave or furlough.

Condensed Milk: A sticky, sweet substance, very different from evaporated milk.

Grappa: A type of Italian brandy. Strega is a liqueur.

Villa: A country home.

Stick: The stick Miss Barkley is carrying is a swagger stick, a useless ornament that British officers sported in World War I. Some United States marine officers carried them until an order banned them.

Somme: A river in France; scene of one of the great battles of World War I, July 1 to November 18, 1916, mainly involving the Germans and the British.

CHAPTER 5

Summary

Lieutenant Henry goes to the bridgehead on the river at Plave to look over conditions so he can plan the best way to use his ambulance unit in the offensive that is planned as soon as a new road is built. In the afternoon, he returns to Gorizia and calls on Miss Barkley, but he is told she is on duty and that he can call after dinner. He does so, and they sit in the garden of the British hospital. Henry tries to make love to her but is rebuffed. But she permits him to kiss her later, and then cries. Henry is puzzled.

Commentary

We are again given a brief description of the war. It is a vivid one, but has little bearing on the main story itself except to re-emphasize that this is a story of people involved in war.

The love story is now being advanced. Henry is on the prowl. We gather that he is not in love with Catherine (the name is brought out for the first time) but would like to have an affair with her. All this is in keeping with his character as it has been drawn before. He has planned his moves and, after Catherine slaps him when he tries to kiss her and then apologizes, he feels that he has it made. Then there is the kiss itself and Catherine's weeping, which puzzles Henry. This is something he had not anticipated. When he returns to his room and Rinaldi teases him, we gather that Henry does not want to talk about the "progress" that Rinaldi says he is making.

This is the first time that we learn the narrator's name is Henry. It is brought out when Miss Ferguson, Miss Barkley's friend, addresses him. Miss Barkley's first name is also revealed in the same manner.

The British attitude toward the Italian army is again brought out, this time by the head nurse at the British hospital when she asks Henry: "You're an American in the Italian army?" There is an air of incredulity about the question. While both the question and the repeated references to the Italian salute and the uniforms may seem to be passing remarks, they do have a bearing on the story.

Notes

A Rivederci: Until we meet again.

Italian Salute: By British and American standards, the manner in which the Italians saluted was somewhat operatic.

Racks of Rockets: These were signal rockets, not the offensive rockets of today.

Metal to Metal Brakes: The story is set in World War I, and trucks of the time had brakes resembling railroad car brakes.

Carabinieri: Italian military police.

Seventy-sevens: Austrian artillery pieces of 77 millimeters, standard field guns.

CHAPTER 6

Summary

Lieutenant Henry is away for two days inspecting the posts. On the evening after his return to Gorizia, he again calls on Catherine Barkley. She asks him if he loves her and he says he does, although he knows he is only playing a game. They sit on a bench in the garden of the hospital. Henry wants to take her elsewhere, but there is no place to go. Catherine tells Henry that she knows he does not mean it when he says he loves her, but that it is all right. Henry thinks that perhaps she is a little crazy. When he returns home, Rinaldi remarks that he is looking puzzled.

Commentary

In this short chapter, Hemingway again stresses that Henry is not in love with Catherine. He is simply on the make. It is nothing but a game, but a game that is better than going to the brothel.

The theme of profane, or non-spiritual, love is still predominant. We see that Catherine is obviously in a highly nervous and distraught state after the death of her fiancé. She needs love, or even Henry's definition of it, and she is receptive to his advances even when she knows what motives lie behind them.

CHAPTER 7

Summary

Henry again goes up to the front to prepare for the offensive that is to start in two days. He has an encounter with a soldier who has a hernia and does not want to rejoin his regiment. The soldier has been to America and speaks English. Henry tries to help him but does not succeed. On returning home, he tries to write a couple of letters before going to dinner. He thinks of the war and wonders what will happen, although he feels that on this front there is little danger of his being killed. He daydreams of taking Catherine Barkley to a hotel in Milan and making love to her. At the mess, he drinks too much and, by the time he remembers to go to the hospital, Catherine has retired for the night. Henry feels "lonely and hollow."

Commentary

The senselessness and dreariness of war is graphically illustrated in this chapter. The soldiers Henry sees are without spirit, weary and tired. The incident of the English-speaking soldier with the hernia has no bearing on the story, although it does illustrate how little enthusiasm most of the participants had for the war.

In the long passage in which he comments on the war, Hemingway is, at this point, telling us that the Austro-Italian front was very different from the front in France. He has brought this out before in Henry's conversation with Catherine about the battle at the Somme, for example, where her fiancé was killed. Henry remarks to himself that he knew he would not be killed, and that the war did not seem to be more dangerous than it was in the movies. At the same time, he voices the wish that it would soon be over. At one point in this reflection, he says: "I could go to Spain if there was no war." This is Hemingway talking. He retained his love for that country to his dying day.

It will become clear later that the key words in this chapter are: "It [the war] did not have anything to do with me." This is an attitude of Henry's that has been brought out before and reinforced in various ways. Both Catherine and Miss Ferguson, for example, find it strange that Henry should be in the Italian army. Henry himself wishes that he were with the British, except that it might be dangerous. This is not necessarily contempt on Hemingway's part toward the Italian army, but his way of establishing that Henry is in a strange position as a "foreigner" in a group so unlike what he is used to.

There were plenty of Americans fighting with the British and, for that matter, French forces, in such outfits as the Lafayette Escadrille, an American-manned flying unit. But, for a lone American to be in the Italian army, on a "strange and mysterious" front, was just that—strange and mysterious. This part of the war story is autobiographical. Hemingway was a Red Cross ambulance driver on the Italian front, and some of the things that happen to Lieutenant Henry later also happened to him. But the love story is probably pure fiction.

Henry's interests are still confined to the physical conquest of Catherine Barkley, as shown in his daydreaming about taking her to a Milan hotel. But, as the chapter ends without his having been able to see her, he has what might be called a sincere emotion toward her for the first time. It is not love, but he does feel "lonely and hollow."

Notes

Smistimento: A clearing station for the wounded.

Fiat: A well-known Italian car and airplane manufacturer.

Brigata: Brigade.

Zona di Guerra: The war zone. These postcards were apparently standard items like birthday greeting telegrams, where the messages were already written.

Hartz Mountains: A mountain group in central Germany, a resort area.

Capri Bianca: A white wine.

Archbishop Ireland: John Ireland (1838-1918) was the first archbishop of St. Paul. He was a strong advocate of total abstinence, an enemy of the liquor traffic, and an opponent of political corruption.

Mistral: A violent, cold and dry northerly wind of the Mediterranean provinces of France.

Bacchus: The Roman god of wine.

CHAPTERS 8, 9

Summary

There is to be an attack that night, so Henry is told to take four ambulances to the area near the river. Before leaving Gorizia he sees Catherine for a moment and she gives him a St. Anthony medallion. When they reach the designated area, they park their cars at a brick-yard where there is a dressing station. In a short time, the offensive starts and Austrian shells are falling in the vicinity. While Henry and his drivers are sitting in a dugout eating cold macaroni and cheese, it is hit by a mortar shell. One of the drivers is killed and Henry is wounded badly in the right leg. The doctors at the dressing station think that he may also have a skull fracture. He is evacuated in one of his own ambulances.

Commentary

Chapter 8 is a very short chapter and is significant only in bringing out the birth of religious feeling between Henry and Catherine, what might be called the turning point from profane to divine love. There is also another of Hemingway's tight and vivid descriptions of the countryside. In one long paragraph he describes a scene that might take many other writers pages.

Chapter 9 is purely a description of the war. Note how the "strange and mysterious" safe front is no longer anything of the sort. War is war, and shells fall on Plava just as they do on the Somme. The mechanics, who are Henry's drivers, have no more interest in the war than he does, but they are involved in it whether they like it or not. The talk in the dugout may be pacifist, but what is going on outside is pure war. When Henry and Gordini return to the dugout from the dressing station with the macaroni and cheese, Manera asks Henry if he was scared. Henry answers: "You're damned right." This is a far cry from the day before when he tells himself that he will be safe on this front.

This distinctively gruesome episode is what makes this not only a great love story but a great war book. The description of the dressing station, the dying driver in the dugout and Henry's own suffering are all brutal and simple. This is war and men are killed. Hemingway is a master at describing war, he pulls no punches.

As the chapter ends, Henry is riding in an ambulance in the dark. Above him, a man is bleeding to death. In the dark come the horrors.

Notes

Saint Anthony: Saint Anthony is the Roman Catholic saint of travellers.

Red Fezzes: A Turkish stovepipe type of cap.

Bersaglieri: Italian mountain troops; considered to be tough fighters.

Observation Balloons: These were used for artillery spotting long before aerial reconnaissance and photography were perfected. They were simply anchored balloons under which a basket was suspended and where an observer sat and watched.

Granatieri: Grenadiers; royal guards picked for their appearance.

Alpini: Mountain troops like the Bersaglieri.

Convert Him: The reference here is to socialism, or perhaps communism. The drivers are mechanics, and in the northern Italian cities such as Milan, Turin and Florence there was—and is—a strong socialist force.

Cognac: French brandy from the Cognac region.

Pasta Asciutta: Dry pasta—noodles.

Four Hundred Twenty or Minnenwerfer: The 420 refers to millimeters, the caliber of a very large howitzer gun. The minnenwerfer was a German trench mortar.

Skoda: A Czechoslovak munitions firm. Czechoslovakia was a part of the Austro-Hungarian Empire at the time.

Porta Feriti: Stretcher bearer. This is the cry of the wounded in every war.

Puttees: A sort of wool bandage that was a part of the uniform of many armies in World War I. It was wound around the legs.

Wallahs: The English ambulance driver had apparently been in India. Wallah means "man" in Hindi, and the English in India often tagged it on to a word, as in "driver-wallah," "bar-wallah," and so forth.

CHAPTERS 10, 11, 12

Summary

Henry is visited at the ward in the field hospital by Rinaldi, who brings him a bottle of brandy and gossip of the town. Rinaldi tells Henry that he does not have a skull fracture and that he will probably get a silver medal for bravery. Later, the priest visits him, bringing some English papers, a bottle of vermouth and mosquito netting. The doctors decide to ship Henry to Milan, where he is to go to the American hospital that has just been installed. The United States has entered the war, but Rinaldi tells Henry that there is still a lack of American nurses and that Catherine will be at the hospital in Milan. As Chapter 12 and Book I ends, Henry is on his way to Milan.

Commentary

We are now coming to the end of Book I, the first encounter with war. Lieutenant Henry has been wounded badly and the interlude of convalescence is to come.

In Chapter 10, Henry is visited in the field hospital by Rinaldi. In Chapter 11, he is visited by the priest. Whether Hemingway did this deliberately or not, the contrast is evident. Rinaldi is cheerful and pleasant, but he brings with him an aura of the brothel and the officers' mess. Rinaldi is by no means an evil man, but he is a man of war. War to him is still an adventure, a chance to further his skills as a surgeon and to make love to the girls. Note how Henry denies it when Rinaldi says that they are really alike underneath. Rinaldi is a friend, but he is also a "war brother."

The priest's visit is very different. He is the man of peace, in contrast to Rinaldi, the man of war. It should be clear by now that Henry wants something more out of life than simply a good time and adventures. He has been wounded in the war and his essential religious feelings come out when he is with the priest. This is not to say that he is a believer in the formal sense, but he is searching for something more than Rinaldi wants.

While Henry says that he does not love very much, in answer to a question from the priest, he does say that: "If I ever get it I will tell you." We are not told what this "it" is, but it is not religion. This "it" is at the core of the book, and it will be brought out as the story progresses.

After the priest leaves, Henry thinks about what the priest had told him about his home country in the mountains. Here, we are again presented with the symbolism of the mountain, the pure place. Hemingway has been showing us, by implication, by use of the priest as a symbol, that Henry is more than just another soldier satisfied with the ordinary pleasures of the flesh.

We are now ready to enter the second stage of this story of war and love. Catherine will be at the American hospital in Milan for which Henry is bound.

Notes

Medaglia d'Argento: Silver medal; a medal for valor.

Coup de Main: Knockout blow.

The *Lancet*: The British Journal of the Royal Medical Society. For a doctor to have an article in it was considered quite an honor.

Kiss Me Good-by: It is not unusual in Latin countries for men to kiss each other on the cheek. It is simply a sign of affection and means nothing more than a grip on the arm might in Anglo-Saxon countries.

Vermouth: A spiced wine. It is the other ingredient in a martini, the first being gin or vodka.

The *News of the World*: A gossipy scandal sheet that is put out in Britain each week. Reputed to have the greatest circulation in the world.

Declaration of War: The United States declared war on Germany on April 2, 1917, but did not declare war on Austria-Hungary until December 7 of the same year.

Scala: The other names mentioned before this are those of restaurants and night clubs in Milan, but the Scala is the famous opera house.

Sight Draft: A draft payable on presentation. What it means here is that Henry writes a cheque that his grandfather will honor back in the U.S.

BOOK II · CHAPTERS 13, 14

Summary

Henry arrives at the American hospital in Milan to discover that he is the first patient. He has not been expected and no doctor is present. He is put in a room where two American nurses, Miss Gage and Mrs. Walker, look after him. He also meets Miss Van Campen, the superintendent, whom he immediately dislikes. He asks Miss Gage if Miss Barkley is here and is told that no such person has arrived yet. The next day, Catherine arrives and, on seeing her, Henry realizes he is in love with her. Although she says she shouldn't because of his wounds, she comes to bed with him for a short time. As the chapter ends we learn that the doctor will be at the hospital in the afternoon.

Commentary

Here, in Chapter 14, for the first time, Henry has sexual relations with Catherine. It is a hurried affair in a hospital room, but it is to be the start of the relationship which is the main theme of this great war novel. Today, when such books as Henry Miller's *Tropic of Cancer* and D. H. Lawrence's *Lady Chatterly's Lover* are readily available, this scene and subsequent love sequences in the novel would be considered tame. But, at the time (1929) that it was published, Henry's affair with Catherine was considered very daring indeed.

While it does not advance the main story in any way, Chapter 13 is a good picture of the monumental snarls that characterize a war. In World War II, the term SNAFU (Situation Normal All Fouled Up) was coined, and this is exactly what Henry runs into. As is generally true of all great writers, Hemingway is able to inject humor into his writing. Here, it is illustrated in his dealings with the confused American nurses and, later, with the Italian barber who thinks he is an Austrian.

Now, the picture changes from Henry's former preoccupation with strictly carnal desires, to the first realization that he is in love. The relationship still involves a strong element of sexuality. When it is over, he says to himself that he had not wanted to fall in love with anyone but he now knew he was. This is the start of the love story.

Notes

Armoire: A large cupboard.

Lake Como: An Italian resort area.

Cinzano: The trade name of a famous vermouth.

Fiasco: An Italian red wine that comes in a wicker container.

CHAPTERS 15, 16, 17

Summary

The next day Henry is taken to the Ospedale Maggiore for X rays. Later, three doctors, whom he considers incompetent, look over the X rays and his legs and tell Henry that they recommend there be a wait of six months before an operation. Henry insists that another doctor be consulted, and Major Valentini comes to see him. He is a cheerful, dynamic character who says he will operate the next day. That night, Catherine stays with him again. After the operation the next day, he is too ill to be interested in her, although she is again on night duty. After that, for several nights Henry and Catherine are together. Eventually, after Miss Ferguson, Catherine's friend, speaks to him about it, Henry asks that she be given a few nights rest. She is gone for three nights and, when she returns to night duty, "It was as though we met again after each of us had been away on a long journey."

Commentary

These are the chapters where the love story is further advanced. Their love is still in the fledgling stage but, by the end of Chapter 17, a certain cohesiveness has been reached. Here, Hemingway is showing that Henry is now definitely in love with Catherine and that it is not simply a carnal affair; tenderness is coming into the story.

The contrast between the incompetent hospital doctors and the volatile Dr. Valentini has nothing much to do with the story, but is an interesting character study. Note that Hemingway identifies the incompetent house doctor with non-alcohol, while Valentini accepts the offer of a drink. In fact, he will "have ten drinks." This is a successful surgeon, a major, not just a first captain. He is presumably a drinking man as compared to the teetotaler who is no good. In Hemingway's world, the good men always drink.

Toward the end of Chapter 17, Henry has conversations with Miss Ferguson and Miss Gage, both friends of Catherine. Note how Miss Ferguson tells Henry not to get Catherine in trouble: "You get her in trouble and I'll kill you." While things are going nicely at the moment, with Henry's leg healing and Catherine by his side, Hemingway is indicating that there is trouble ahead. Tragedy is always hovering nearby in this great war novel.

Notes

Ospedale Maggiore: The Main Hospital; the top Italian military hospital in Milan.

Cheery Oh, Cheery Oh: Dr. Valentini is saying what he believes all British say when they drink. The normal spelling of this British expression is "Cheerio," and has nothing to do with drinking. Cheerio is somewhat equivalent to our "so-long" or "be seeing you."

CHAPTERS 18, 19, 20

Summary

During the summer Henry convalesces in Milan. He and Catherine are together a great deal of the time. Henry tells Catherine he wants to marry her as soon as possible but she points out that if they marry she will be sent back to Britain and that it is not cosy for foreigners to get married in Italy in these troubled times. The summer goes by without much happening. Henry, Catherine and others that they meet spend a pleasant, uneventful summer far from the fighting.

Commentary

This is the summer interlude that is to come before the storms of autumn. There are no important developments that advance the story. But this is not a plotted novel in the sense that there is a hero and a villain. There is a villain, but the villains are war, evil and the things of the night. The hero is not Frederic Henry and the heroine is not Catherine Barkley, but love. Here, Hemingway advances the latter theme. Henry is anxious to marry Catherine, but she is the one who tells him that she is already married to him as far as she is concerned.

Again, it is brought out that when Henry first met Catherine, she was a deeply troubled woman. Now, she says: "But now we're happy and we love each other." That is enough for Catherine and, in a sense, it is enough for Henry. Hemingway indicates that while he "really" wants to marry Catherine, he supposed he "enjoyed not being married really." This is still in the foundation stage of their love, however, and this feeling will change as the story progresses.

There are incidents in these chapters in which Henry meets various characters. There is the couple, Mr. and Mrs. Meyers, whom Hemingway indicates left the United States under some sort of a cloud. But this is never explained. There is Ettore Moretti, an Italian from San Francisco, now a captain in the Italian Army, who is what might be called a professional hero. And there are the two American students of opera. All this is simply ice cream on the cake of the story, and adds nothing but taste to the main dish. In all of Hemingway's novels, these human touches are inserted.

Toward the end of Chapter 19, there is a significant interlude. Henry and Catherine are in his room in the hospital when it begins to rain, building gradually to a torrential downpour. The symbolism of the rain, which has only been hinted at so far, is now brought out clearly. Catherine asks Henry if he will always love her as he says he will, then she says: "That's good. Because I'm afraid of the rain."

Henry is not particularly impressed by this and tells her he will love her in any kind of weather. In fact, in the short dialogue that follows, the impression is that Henry simply wants to go to sleep but is humoring the girl he loves. Then Catherine says: "I'm afraid of the rain because sometimes I see me dead in it." Henry tells her that she is simply imagining things and he comforts her, but the sense of tragedy that hangs over the book is again brought out in contrast to the happy summer days the lovers are spending together.

Notes

Marsala: An Italian wine somewhat like sherry.

Threw the Benches: The ordinary Italian is a fervent opera-lover and, for him, opera is not a formal affair. The front rows at the Scala Opera House are benches and it is said that when they don't like a performer, the audience gets up and throws the benches on the stage.

Potato Masher: The Germans and Austrians used a hand grenade that had a handle below the grenade proper. It looked something like a potato masher.

Enough Rank: Things were not very democratic in World War I and, even in the United States, only officers were admitted to the better restaurants. The reference here is to the fact that Henry is a second lieutenant but, with enough rank, as Catherine puts it, to be admitted to the better restaurants.

Tramway: Tram is British for "streetcar."

CHAPTERS 21, 22, 23, 24

Summary

In September, Henry is coming to the end of his stay in the hospital in Milan. He learns that the war is going very badly and that there is a possibility that German troops will be used on the Italian front. One day, on returning to the hospital, he finds official orders telling him that he will have three weeks convalescent leave, starting October 4, after which he is to return to the front. Further, Catherine tells him that she is three months pregnant. Henry loses his convalescent leave, however, because he comes down with a case of jaundice. The superintendent of nurses, Miss Van Campen, finds various liquor bottles in his room. She accuses him of drinking to get jaundice as a means to avoid returning to the front. Henry indignantly denies this, but he spends two weeks in bed and ultimately loses his leave. The night that Henry has to leave for the front, he and Catherine go to a hotel near the railway station and rent a room. Catherine is unhappy, but she is brave at the same time and tells Henry not to worry about her. They take a carriage to the railway station and say good-bye in the rain. Henry boards the train and starts back to the front.

Commentary

In contrast to the summer chapters, these are the autumn chapters. The mood of happiness that has been built up is abruptly changed. Everything is different: the weather, the conditions at the front and the situation between Henry and Catherine.

In Chapter 21, we are told that the summer was gone and that "the fighting at the front went very badly." Then, when Henry returns to the hospital, Catherine tells him that she is three months pregnant. Also, he receives the news that he is to return to the front after three weeks convalescent leave, but this does not materialize because he comes down with jaundice and has a fight with Miss Van Campen over the liquor bottles in his room. The leave is cancelled.

Nothing goes right for Henry or Catherine in this section of the book. Even on the last night the two lovers have together when they go to a hotel, the room they are given is so sleazy that Catherine says she feels like a whore. But, in time, this feeling passes and the symbolism of home that is ever present when the two are together is brought out again: "After we had eaten we felt fine, and then after, we felt very happy and in a little time the room felt like our home again. My room at the hospital had been our home and this room was our home too in the same way."

The parting between Henry and Catherine is a simple and pathetic one. In its lack of histrionics lies its power. Hemingway deliberately underplays what might well be the final parting of the lovers—one who is going off to war and the other who is going to have an illegitimate child. When Henry asks Catherine how she feels, she says simply that she is "sleepy." At the station, there is no crying when they part and after the carriage takes off, Catherine leans out, "smiled and waved." But note that all this occurs while it is raining, the symbol of tragedy.

The summer of contentment is over and the autumn of truth has arrived as Book II ends.

Notes

San Gabriele: A mountain in what is now Yugoslavia; the scene of intense battles in World War I.

Rioting: As mentioned before, workers in Turin rioted against continuation of the ruinous war. This was in 1917.

Cooked: English slang for "had it" or "finished."

Balls: English slang (obscene) for nonsense.

Hun: English term in World War I for the Germans; also known as the Boche.

Babe Ruth: It should be noted that the greatest home-run hitter of them all was originally a pitcher, and a very good one at that.

Jaundice: A liver disease referred to nowadays as hepatitis. The victim turns yellow, cannot eat or drink and is in considerable discomfort.

Kummel: An anise-flavored liqueur.

Platform Tickets: In many foreign countries, it is necessary to purchase—at a small price—platform tickets in order to see people off at the railway station.

Rucksack: A knapsack, like the ones hikers carry on their backs.

Larks: The Italians kill and eat all manner of little songbirds. They are considered a delicacy.

Capri and St. Estephe: Italian wines.

Woodcock: A game bird, highly esteemed by gourmets.

Soufflé Potatoes: Mashed potatoes whipped up with eggs and baked.

Puree de Marron: Mashed chestnuts, a great delicacy in haute cuisine.

Zabaione: An Italian dessert that consists of egg yolk and various liqueurs.

Musette: A bag that was slung over one shoulder and favored by officers in World War I.

Compartment: The set-up of Italian trains was, and is, somewhat different from ours. A narrow corridor runs along the length of the car, and off this are a number of compartments where the seats face each other.

BOOK III · CHAPTERS 25, 26

Summary

Henry returns to his old headquarters in Gorizia. He reports to the major and later talks at length with his room-mate, Rinaldi. It appears that the war is going badly and, while neither the major nor Rinaldi thinks that the Austrians will attack this late in the year, there is no confidence of victory. Later, at the mess, none of the officers Henry formerly knew were there, and it is presumed that they are dead. The priest arrives and Rinaldi baits him, but there is no sting in his remark. Rinaldi goes off to the town and the priest talks with Henry in his room. The priest is depressed at the way things are going.

Commentary

Nothing particularly significant happens in these two chapters in which Henry returns to his old headquarters in Gorizia, but a careful reading will reveal a great deal about the feelings of men who have been at war much too long. All the pep has gone out of the combatants. The major is "older and drier," Rinaldi "looked tired" and the priest, while outwardly the same, says, "It has been a terrible summer."

There is a good deal of dialogue in these two chapters. In fact, it is almost all dialogue, and a very good example of Hemingway's masterful use of it. When Henry and Rinaldi talk, it is the banter of good friends even though they are from two very different cultures. We can see that behind the façade that the playboy, Rinaldi, wears, he is truly a dedicated surgeon and essentially a very decent and good man. Even when Rinaldi baits the priest, it is only because it is part of the game, and the priest, the major and Henry know this. In this there is tragedy, for Rinaldi is now only a shell of what he was. When the major says that Rinaldi "thinks" he has syphilis, it is simply that. We never do find out if Rinaldi is really physically stricken. We do know that he is stricken in the soul and he apparently convinces himself that he is also stricken physically. It is all part of the sickness of war that Hemingway is conveying.

These are what might be called sick chapters. There is deliberately no life portrayed in them. They are a lead-in to what is more than sickness: death.

Notes

Caporetto: A town in Gorizia Province, now in Yugoslavia. It is on the Isonzo River.

Bainsizza: A plateau north of Gorizia.

Rinin: Most European languages have standard diminutive names just as in English. Richard becomes Dick and, in Italian, Rinin is the diminutive of Rinaldi.

Rinaldo, Purissimo, Sporchissimo: Purest Rinaldi, dirtiest Rinaldi.

Bosnia: Today a part of Yugoslavia, it was ruled by the Turks for several centuries; the inhabitants are mostly Muslims.

CHAPTERS 27, 28

Summary

Henry goes up to the front at Bainsizza and rejoins his old ambulance unit. That night, in the midst of a rainstorm, the Austrians, or Germans, if the rumors are to be believed, attack and the Italians fall back. The next night, the retreat starts and Henry hears that the Austrians and Germans have broken through in the north and are coming down the mountain valleys. He is ordered to take his three ambulances and evacuate the field hospitals and take the hospital equipment. During all this time it is raining steadily. "The retreat was orderly, wet and sullen." Henry arrives back at his old headquarters in Gorizia to find that everyone has left. He takes his men into the villa and they have a short sleep before continuing on the retreat, which is now taking on larger proportions. Civilians in carts and on foot have joined the procession, and somewhere along the line the ambulances pick up two teenage girls and two engineer sergeants. The road to Udine is so congested that Henry realizes he will have to take off across country if he is ever to reach his destination. He orders the ambulances to turn off on a side road. At a deserted farmhouse they find some cheese and wine before proceeding further.

Commentary

These two chapters mark Hemingway's masterful description of one of the biggest retreats in history. The Austrians and Germans began their drive on October 24, 1917, under the command of General Otto von Bulow. The Italian troops commanded by General Cadorna fell back. Note that in these chapters the retreat is still orderly, although the disintegration is starting as we get into Chapter 28.

The key to the war situation in these chapters is the word "Germans." This is the first time that the Germans have entered the war on the Italian front and, as Henry says: "The word Germans was something to be frightened of. We did not want to have anything to do with the Germans."

There are several interesting characters who appear in these chapters. The two engineer sergeants and the two girls serve as simply window dressing to the main thrust of the story, showing the types of people involved in the war. Again, we see contrasts of the good and the bad, the pure and the evil. This will become plainer later.

Notes

Dolce: Literally, "sweet." In this case, a dessert.

Croats and Magyars: The old Austro-Hungarian Empire contained many ethnic types. The Croats came from Croatia, which is now a part of Yugoslavia. They were tough fighters. The Magyars are Hungarians.

Barbera: An Italian wine. There is a great deal of wine drinking in this book, but it should be remembered that to an Italian or a Frenchman or a Spaniard, wine is almost always served with meals.

Tagliamento: A river in northern Italy. It plays an important part in this novel.

Sorelia: Sister.

Dialect: The two girls speak a dialect that none of Henry's group can understand. The common misapprehension that there is such a language as "Italian" or "Spanish" or "German" does not apply among uneducated rural people, who speak dialects that may not be understood 100 miles away.

CHAPTERS 29, 30

Summary

Shortly after Henry's three ambulances leave the farmhouse, one of them gets stuck in the mud. They all go to work to free it, but the two engineer sergeants start off on their own. Henry orders them to help and when they refuse and keep on going he shoots at them, killing one of them. Later, they become completely stalled and decide to walk to Udine. Henry gives the girls some money and tells them to rejoin the people on the road. He and his group go across the fields. They come to a river and discover that one bridge has been blown up but the two others are intact. On one they see a German staff car and bicycle troops crossing, going in the direction of Udine. After Henry and his men cross the bridge, they try to stay under cover, but one of his men is shot and killed, and Henry suspects it is the Italian rear guard who did it. Another of his men deserts him. Henry and his one remaining soldier find a deserted farmhouse and something to eat and drink. After a short rest they take off again into the night. They make it to a road and join troops and civilians who are in full and confused retreat. After they cross the Tagliamento River, Henry is arrested by military police who suspect him of being a German in Italian uniform. The military—or battle—police are dealing out death sentences on the spot, so Henry decides to make a break for it. He runs for the flooded river, dives in and manages to hang on to a piece of timber that floats by.

Commentary

Now the tempo of the retreat and of the war is going into high gear. Note that Chapter 29 starts almost immediately with violence when Henry shoots one of the engineer sergeants. When Bonello, one of Henry's drivers, finishes the job of killing the sergeant, it is only another indication of how chaos has taken over from reason.

This theme builds up rapidly. The killing of Aymo by his own countryman is just another indication of the senselessness and confusion of war. Bonello's desertion and desire to be taken a prisoner, rather than die, is equally senseless. And, finally, the ultimate insanity is illustrated by the actions of the battle police. Some critics say that Hemingway is showing that Henry is now faced with military justice akin to that he had so summarily dealt the sergeant.

The scenes Hemingway has depicted in the previous chapters, on the retreat from Caporetto, now build up to a climax. There is almost complete confusion: the soldiers cursing all officers, the cries of "Hooray for peace," the discarding of arms, the inane battle police dealing out their kangaroo-court justice. This is the Great Retreat, and it is possibly the best description of military chaos since Tolstoy's description of the Grand Armee's retreat from Moscow in *War and Peace*. The whole atmosphere of the retreat is one of confusion and anarchy. This is no longer the "picturesque front" mentioned in the early chapters, but a nightmarish scene of complete war.

Several critics have commented on Henry's dive into the river as a symbolic thing. Malcolm Cowley has likened Henry's plunge into the river to escape as a baptism, a symbol of his entering the world of the initiated. Carlos Baker also finds it significant as an indication that Henry is washing himself of the past, of the war in which he does not really have any interest. Whether the author himself intended symbolism of this type is not known, of course, but critics have dissected Hemingway's writings in several books and dozens of articles. In any case, his plunge into the river ends one phase of this war book.

Notes

Cock It: Readers may not know that an automatic pistol must be cocked—that is to say, the bullet put into the firing chamber—before it will go off.

Imola: A city in northern Italy. As mentioned before, the workingmen in the northern Italian industrial areas were, and are, supporters of the leftist movements.

Sausage: The sausage referred to here is a salami and not a frankfurter or link sausage; salami will keep much longer.

Sealing Wax: A largely unknown product today, used only to affix seals to solemn international treaties, but quite common many years ago and used to seal letters and other documents from prying eyes. In this case, it is used in addition to the cork to keep air out of the wine.

A Basso Gli Ufficiali: This and subsequent other Italian expressions are explained. This one means "down with the officers."

Battle Police: Military police near the front who were authorized to mete out justice to deserters and others.

CHAPTERS 31, 32

Summary

Henry hangs on to his timber and is carried down the river in the swift current. At one time he almost drowns. At about dawn, he makes it to shore. Once on shore, he cuts the officer's stars off his sleeve and takes off across country. He comes to a railway and manages to get aboard a freight train and hide under the canvas on an open car that is carrying guns. He hurts his head, but not badly. Henry is very hungry, wet and tired and he lies on the floor of the flatcar wishing that it will get to Mestre so he can get off and find a place to eat. He thinks of Catherine and tells himself that he will take her some place away from the war. As far as he is concerned, he is through with it. The treatment he received from the battle police has convinced him of that.

Commentary

These are the chapters that gave birth to the title. Henry is through with war and is making his own farewell to arms.

In Chapter 31, Hemingway does not dwell on Henry's thoughts in any great detail. Henry is too involved in keeping alive to be doing much abstract thinking. But after he gets on the train, he has time to reflect on the things that have happened.

"Anger was washed away in the river along with any obligation," Henry says. He goes on to explain that all that had ceased when the *carabiniere* had put his hands on his collar at the inspection point. We gather that Henry has done his share of fighting for the Italians, who are an alien people to him. He was, we also gather, prepared to do more, but when they treated him with preposterous injustice, he had had it. As he says, he was not against them, he was simply through.

Note that this theme has been dwelt on for some time. What on earth is he doing in the Italian army, the English nurses want to know? There is a difference, we are led to understand, between an American deserting from the Italian army and an American deserting from the United States army. There is no sense of guilt on Henry's part. While he does not say it, we are led to believe that he has done all he can do, and now he feels he can do no more.

This ends Henry's active role in the war. But the war is still going on and its influence on the protagonists remains.

Practically everything in these chapters is self-explanatory except the rather involved geographical locations. All the names given, such as Mestre, San Vito and Pordenone are towns in northern Italy in the plains below the Alps. Henry is trying to get to Milan, and these are places he must pass through or around.

BOOK IV · CHAPTERS 33, 34, 35, 36

Summary

Henry drops off the train in Milan early in the morning and goes to a coffee shop near the station. The proprietor recognizes that he is in trouble and offers to help him, but Henry refuses. He then goes to the hospital and learns from the porter that Catherine has gone to Stresa. From the hospital he goes to the apartment of an American who is studying singing in Italy. Simmons, the singer, offers Henry civilian clothing, and also tells him that if he goes to Switzerland, he will be free to move about. After getting into civilian clothes, Henry takes a train for Stresa, a resort town on Lake Maggiore. On arriving, he goes to a hotel and asks if Catherine is there. He discovers that she is at another hotel and surprises Catherine and Miss Ferguson by walking in on them while they are eating dinner. Miss Ferguson is very angry at Henry for what she calls his "sneaky" ways and for having got Catherine in trouble. When Henry and Catherine are alone they talk things over and decide that they must go to Switzerland, which is across the lake. Catherine is worried that the Italian authorities will catch up with Henry. For two days the lovers find life at the hotel on the lake most pleasant. Henry goes fishing with the bartender and he meets an old friend, the venerable Count Greffi, and plays billiards with him. But, on the second night, the bartender knocks on their door and tells Henry that he will be arrested in the morning and must take off immediately for Switzerland. He offers to loan them his rowboat. Henry, seeing no alternative, thanks him and takes up the offer. The bartender gets them sandwiches and something to drink, and Henry and Catherine get in the boat in the middle of the night, in the rain, to row about 20 miles across the lake to Switzerland. The lake is rough, for there has been a storm earlier.

Commentary

These are what might be called the "civilian interlude in Italy" chapters. Things start off well with the offer of help from the coffee-shop proprietor, the kindness of the hospital porter and his wife, and the assistance he receives from the American, Simmons.

In Stresa, the lovers are reunited and, except for Miss Ferguson's blast at their immoral conduct—as she views it—there is a brief interlude of peace and happiness. We gather that, at some former period, Henry has been at Stresa on several occasions, for he is friendly with the bartender at the hotel and with the venerable Count Greffi. Count Greffi is possibly a symbol of what Hemingway considered a gracious age that was now past. Aside from some rather philosophic observations, he plays no active part in the story, whereas the bartender very definitely does.

In Chapter 34, there is a passage that has been much quoted, and perhaps sums up Hemingway's thinking about the love of a man for a woman. This touching passage starts: "That night at the hotel . . ." and goes on: "Often a man wishes to be alone and a girl wishes to be alone too and if they love each other they are jealous of that in each other, but I can truly say we never felt that. We could feel alone when we were together, alone against the others . . . I know that the night is not the same as the day: that all things are different, that the things of the night cannot be explained in the day, because they do not then exist, and the night can be a dreadful time for lonely people once their loneliness has started . . ."

There is more to it, but this is a key passage. In many of Hemingway's other writings he has spoken of the horrors of the night for those who are alone, physically or spiritually. In this case, it also goes to point out what Carlos Baker calls the "home and not-home," of this novel. Where Catherine is, is "home," and where she is not is "not home," according to this critic.

In the rain, Henry and Catherine head toward Switzerland. Again, it is the intervention of an ordinary Italian that makes this possible, for it is the bartender that wakes them, gives them his boat and sends them on their way. Hemingway always writes with the greatest respect of the little man, and here is a case in point.

Notes

Stresa: A town on the west shore of Lake Maggiore. It is in a resort area. The border of Italy and Switzerland runs through the lake. Stresa has been the scene of several international conferences: in 1935, the representatives of Italy, Great Britain and France met there in an effort to show united opposition to the rearmament of Germany. History shows us that the conference was not what could be called an outstanding success.

Letto Matrimoniale: Matrimonial bed.

Borghese: Civilian clothes.

Mufti: This is the English expression for soldiers in civilian clothes. Khaki is uniform, mufti not.

Cortina d'Ampezzo: A mountain resort, famous for skiing. The 1956 Winter Olympic Games were held there.

Metternich: Prince Klemens von Metternich (1773-1859); Austrian statesman.

Fifteen Points in a Hundred: A normal game of billiards—not pool—is a hundred points. The reference here is to a handicap.

Five Hundred Francs: The barman is talking about Swiss francs, a desirable medium of exchange. This was worth about $100, American.

Thirty Five Kilometers: A kilometer is 0.62 miles. A handy rule of thumb is to multiply by six and drop off the last digit. Thus, six times thirty five comes to 210 or in this case, 21 miles.

CHAPTER 37

Summary
Henry rows all night on Lake Maggiore. While he is afraid they will be caught by a customs boat, they finally arrive in Switzerland. After having breakfast in a Swiss village, Henry and Catherine are arrested and taken to the city of Locarno where they are questioned by the authorities. But, because they have money and passports, they are released. Catherine decides that she wants to go to Montreux, but before they do they put up at a hotel for the night. Both of them are exhausted from the ordeal on the lake.

Commentary
This is the escape from Italy chapter. There is nothing particularly dramatic about it, although at one point there is a danger that Henry and Catherine will be caught by customs agents. Even though Henry is working very hard rowing the boat, there is a certain sense of cheerfulness throughout the episode, as though both he and Catherine know that they will make it safely.

When the two finally arrive at the Swiss village in the morning, the first words that Catherine says illustrate the feeling of escape: "What a lovely country." She goes on to say how good it feels under her shoes. All this is before they have seen anything of it. But the sense of relief at getting away from what Henry calls "that bloody place" is all-prevailing. Even the rain that Catherine hates so much is a "cheerful" rain.

Nothing that happens to them in their encounter with the authorities changes this mood of cheerfulness. Henry and Catherine are treated by the Swiss in the typical Swiss pragmatic way. The Swiss are full of practical virtues, and one of them is that any money brought into the country and spent is a boon to their economy. Note how Henry says the Swiss lieutenant was "favorably impressed" when he discovered that Henry had twenty-five hundred lira on him and Catherine twelve hundred. Later, in Locarno, the same thing happens. They are "polite because we had passports and money." This is not a criticism on Hemingway's part of either Switzerland or the Swiss, but a rather humorous illustration of the Swiss character. He brings this out in some of his short stories.

Now, Henry and Catherine have made their escape and the war phase of the novel is definitely over. In contrast to the horror of war, they are starting a happy life together.

Notes

Feather the Oars: This is a way of twisting the wrist and flattening the oar blade to a parallel position to the water on the return stroke.

Backed Water: Using one oar to go forward and the other to reverse, a way of turning quickly.

Guardia di Finanza: Literally, finance guards, customs officers.

Catch Crabs: In rowing, to catch one's oar in the water on the back stroke before completing it. It holds up the advance considerably and in a crew race can be disastrous.

Provisional Visa: A visa is stamp on one's passport indicating that the country of the visa's origin will let one enter. A provisional visa is just what Henry explains it is.

BOOK V · CHAPTERS 38, 39, 40

Summary

Henry and Catherine take rooms in a house above Montreux. They have the upper floor of a small tavern owned by a Swiss couple who have been in the hotel business and are now retired. They spend the fall and winter months there and are very happy. They are far from the war, and they enjoy walks by the lake and occasionally go into Montreux. Catherine's pregnancy is proceeding without difficulties. As Henry says, "We had a fine life." In March, Catherine's time is approaching, so they move into Lausanne where the hospital is located. They go to a hotel and find it very pleasant.

Commentary

These are the happy chapters, the contented chapters. Everything that happens is an indication of how Hemingway feels people should live. The rooms the lovers have are warm and pleasant and, from the window, they can see the lake and the mountains. Hemingway's powers of description are very evident here when he describes the location of the chalet and the country around it. The descriptions are not long, for Hemingway is never verbose, but they sing, and it is a very good example of the writer's singularly masterful way of setting the scene. It is doubtful if any other writer is able to describe a setting as simply as Hemingway and yet at the same time paint it as vividly. The first chapter of this book is one example. The few paragraphs in these chapters are another. This "feeling for the country" has been commented on by many critics.

The critic, Carlos Baker, in his book *Hemingway, The Writer as Artist,* who strongly advances the mountain (good) and plains (bad) symbolism in this book says of this interlude: "Soon they are settled into a supremely happy life in the winterland on the mountainside above Montreux." It is, he adds, ". . . the closest approximation of the priest's fair homeland in the Abruzzi that they are ever to know."

On one visit into Montreux, Henry and Catherine talk about getting married, but it is Catherine who says she wants to wait until she is "thin" again. As they are sitting and drinking beer in a cafe, Catherine says: "The doctor said I was rather narrow in the hips and it's all for the best if we keep young Catherine small."

Henry is concerned and asks a few more questions, but the matter is then dropped. This is a significant point, however, and should be borne in mind.

In the spring, the rains start and the lovers move out of the house in which they have been so happy. They move into a hotel in Lausanne—which is in the plains. "It was not bad," Henry says, but, on the other hand, it is nothing like what they had in Montreux.

As the chapters end, there is another famous Hemingway phrase that has often been quoted: "We knew the baby was very close now and it gave us both a feeling as though something were hurrying us and we could not lose any time together."

The happy mood is ending and the "something" that is hurrying them will become very evident shortly.

Notes

Porcelain Stove: It is exactly that, a large affair of porcelain, common in parts of Europe.

Hoyle: Hoyle's book of rules is the standard book for all disputes in card games.

Munich Beer: Beer from Munich is considered by many to be the finest in the world.

Chamois: A small goatlike antelope that lives in the Alps. The skin is highly valued. Shammy, or chammy, however, is seldom made from chamois skin any more. It is more likely to come from a sheep.

Lausanne: A city on the north shore of the Lake of Geneva.

CHAPTER 41

Summary

Catherine's labor pains start and Henry takes her to the hospital. Catherine's pains become progressively worse but the baby does not come. Henry goes to a cafe for a quick breakfast. When he returns to the hospital Catherine is still in labor and very much worse. At two o'clock in the afternoon, when he returns to the cafe for lunch, Catherine is still in labor and suffering badly. Late in the afternoon the doctor tells Henry that he recommends a Caesarean section as the only solution. Henry agrees. Later, surgeons arrive, and Catherine is taken into surgery. The baby is born dead, but Henry only learns of this from the nurse later. He does not tell Catherine. The nurse tells Henry that Catherine is all right and suggests he go and have supper. Henry again goes to the same cafe. When he returns to the hospital, he discovers that Catherine has had a hemorrhage and is in very serious condition. Catherine tells Henry she is not afraid, but she knows that she is dying. The hemorrhages continue and "it did not take her very long to die." Henry chases everyone out of the room. "It was like saying good-bye to a statue." He walks back to the hotel in the rain.

Commentary

Now the whole mood that has been built up changes. The happy days in Switzerland are abruptly coming to an end. From the moment that Catherine's labors start, we can feel an element of doom. She suffers horribly, but bravely, and Henry suffers with her.

After Henry has his breakfast and leaves the cafe, he sees a dog nosing in a garbage can. Henry looks in and sees only coffee grounds. "There isn't anything, dog," he says, and this sets the mood for what is to come.

This is a masterfully designed chapter. It piles emotion on emotion until it reaches an almost unbearable height of tragedy. Catherine's labor pains that grow worse and worse are the foundation. "Give it to me. Give it to me," she cries, reaching for the laughing gas. Then the doctor tells Henry that: "It doesn't go," and we are prepared for what is to come. The Caesarean, the dead baby and then the hemorrhage.

Hemingway injects into this chapter a great deal of his philosophy. The key sentences are possibly: "So now they got her in the end. You never get away with anything." And Catherine says: "I'm not brave any more, darling. I'm all broken. They've broken me. I know it now.'' But she is brave to the end, as are all of Hemingway's heroines. This bravery compounds the tragedy.

Here is a tragic and classic chapter, possibly the saddest in the sense of emotion, that the great modern tragedian ever wrote. Every one of Hemingway's novels is a tragedy, and there are some tremendous final chapters in such books as *For Whom the Bell Tolls,* when Robert Jordan lies dying on a hill in Spain; but for sheer, naked tragedy, the final chapter in *A Farewell to Arms* probably beats them all.

Carlos Baker, the critic, has this to say:

> Her [Catherine's] death exactly completes the symbolic structure, the edifices of tragedy so carefully erected . . . It is achieved without obvious insistence of belaboring of the point, but it is indubitably achieved for any reader who has found his way into the heart of the book. And it is this achievement which enables Hemingway's first study in doom to succeed as something far more than an exercise in romantic naturalism.

The symbolism that Baker and others speak of is evident here. The death takes place in the plains. Note that when Henry finally leaves the hospital he ''walked back to the hotel in the rain.''

Notes
Brioche: A pastry, eaten for breakfast in some European countries.

Gas: Laughing gas, nitrous oxide, used as an anesthetic; so-called from the reaction it may produce.

Kirsch, Marc: Kirsch is an anise-flavored liqueur, Marc a brandy.

Choucroute: French sauerkraut; pickled cabbage.

Plat du Jour: Plate of the day; the special for the day.

Pile of Saucers: This is a custom in France and some other European countries. All drinks are brought on saucers and the saucers are left. When the time comes for payment, the waiter counts up the saucers.

Character Sketches

Frederic Henry

Frederic Henry, the narrator and main character in *A Farewell to Arms,* is a lieutenant in the ambulance corps of the Italian army. He is clearly a young man capable of eliciting affection from others, though he is not overly affectionate himself. He treats everyone with courtesy—the barman, his orderlies, the old Roman Count—and with a sort of understated warmth. His reaction to the war situation is a kind of detached stoicism, informed by a more profound awareness of the darkness of reality. Unlike Jake, in *The Sun Also Rises,* Henry is an active participant in the events of his time. Also unlike Jake, Henry undergoes significant changes in his attitude during the period covered by the novel. From a position of somewhat unthinking commitment, Frederic Henry goes to increased bitterness and final disinvolvement—the separate peace of desertion from social chaos and madness.

Henry's experiences are partly based on the events that lead to the severe wounds Hemingway sustained on July 8, 1918. Henry's relationship with Rinaldi in Gorizia is the world of two men sharing a male camaraderie. It is, in its way, a sort of blissful world the two share, which will not be repeated later in the book. In interesting contrast with Hemingway's own choice of marriage partners—who were often involved in the craft of writing—there is little sharing of active interest between Henry and Catherine Barkley. They play all kinds of two-handed card games while waiting for the child's birth, but there are no indications of any potential dual activities for the two lovers. As a matter of fact, we are not clearly informed about Henry's hobbies or interests. In addition, no information about his past is given in the novel. The lieutenant is peculiarly restless. His participation in the war, which he comes to detest and despise, constitutes just about the only context for his being.

Frederic Henry is a lonesome and confused man. One of the first images of the novel depicts him as a man wandering from one brothel to another, incapable of discovering any meaning in life. In conversations with the priest from Abruzzi, Henry hears about the cold, clear, dry country of the mountains and associates that country with an ordered and disciplined life. Apparently, Henry does not function well in the whirlwind existence of disorder and confusion. His basic desire to derive some code of life can be seen as the motive that first prompts him to pursue Catherine. His reactions to Catherine are at first physical, since he would prefer to sleep with her than to go to the army brothels. But, as he becomes more and more involved with Catherine, he sees in their relationship a type of order, a type of commitment to a regular existence.

Having discovered this basic value in his relationship with Catherine, Henry returns to the front and sees the Italian army in total disorder and confusion. He realizes that he can no longer remain a part of this large group. When the small group to which he had felt such loyalty disperses, and when Frederic Henry sees members of the Italian army trying and executing their own soldiers on trumped-up charges of desertion, Henry decides that the time has come to desert. Henry's desertion can be justified on the grounds that he is loyal only to a small group and that he is searching for order and discipline in life. When he sees the Italian army in chaos, he feels no more allegiance to what has become an abstract organization. In contrast, he feels a deep sense of loyalty to Catherine. In the love they have for each other, he can discover a sense of duty, a sense of order, and can develop a code by which he can live.

Malcolm Cowley has described Hemingway as one of the "haunted and nocturnal" writers in the American literary tradition. Occasional interludes that take place at times when Henry is near sleep constitute as near a return to the past as the reader is likely to get in the novel. "I slept heavily except once I woke sweating and scared and then went back to sleep trying to stay outside of my dream . . . once it was really light I went back to sleep again." Lieutenant Henry does not attempt to analyze his anxieties. Rarely, in fact, does he allow them to come fully to consciousness. This general "stoicism" seems to exist even in his subconscious.

It would be wrong, however, to conclude that Henry lacks a capacity for enjoying life. That he has such a capacity is demonstrated not only by his closeness to Catherine—and his pleasure in that closeness—but also in his pleasantly aimless conversations with various minor characters. He responds favorably to those aspects in people that join them in the appreciation of simple goodness and more earthy matters like good food and drink. And it is to this quality that the reader tends to respond most directly.

Catherine Barkley

Catherine Barkley is a static character. By this we mean that she is the same at the end of the novel as she was at the beginning. In one sense, her function is to gauge the extent of the development seen in Frederic Henry. From the beginning of the novel, we see that Catherine understands the finality of death, yet Henry does not recognize it until the end of the novel. Furthermore, we see that it is Catherine who represents the rejection of traditional values. She does not want to be married, even though Henry has suggested it. And, although there are practical reasons for this, Catherine realizes that marriage is just another empty form and is therefore meaningless. Similarly, when Henry speaks of having the child baptized, Catherine Barkley sees no need for this.

In an essay setting forth some interesting similarities between the women in the works of Hemingway and Kipling, Edmund Wilson emphasizes the frequent recurrence of a type of female character that Catherine represents. The sort of woman who is docile and all-accepting also appears in some Kipling stories as the obedient native consort of a number of British officials. Maria, the heroine of *For Whom the Bell Tolls,* is much like Catherine Barkley, and both are akin to Wilson's model of the submissive woman. Nevertheless, these women are important to character analysis in that they tend to emphasize the author's procedure in presenting the hero of the novel. It can hardly be argued that Catherine's is a particularly believable or realistic portrayal. Even such an apologist for the ''stable heroine'' and the ''moral norm of womanly behavior'' as Carlos Baker does not deny the degree of abstraction that constitutes Catherine Barkley. Since Hemingway's novelistic heroes tend to want to ''go it alone,'' their choice of women is often not unreasonable. In addition, the woman who might complicate this desire by strong counter-wishes is likely to distort the quality of the world that Hemingway wishes to portray.

Catherine is young and attractive. She is presented in the beginning of the novel as still immersed in the dislocation of personality that results from a grievous personal loss: her fiancé had been killed in the war. What started out as a casual wartime affair in *A Farewell to Arms* is transformed into a love that returns to her a sense of the beauty and significance of life. Her devotion and concern for her lover are absolute. She takes all the night shifts—the most taxing—in the hospital to be near Henry. When there is a question of her accompanying her lover on a leave, it is clear that no professional commitment to nursing will be able to keep her from going with him. For Henry, she is that unique human being whose essential power consists in the ability to make a home out of the most rigidly uncompromising places (a strange hotel room, a hospital sickbed, an isolated chalet). She has no pleasure but in her lover, no thoughts or life outside of his.

Catherine Barkley has made a religion out of her love for Henry. What physical description there is of her suggests that she represents the eternally feminine woman. She is perfectly content to devote herself solely to the man she loves. She has already confronted the reality of death when she lost her fiancé. And she has arrived at the conviction that life and its pleasures are the most important of all things.

Catherine Barkley's response to her own imminent death indicates the stature she has attained as a character. Some critics have suggested that Catherine died a noble and stoic death. A more accurate judgment might be that Catherine died as she had lived, nobly and stoically. Her view of her own death is clearly expressed in her statement, ''It's just a dirty trick.'' She realizes that, with death, she is losing all the pleasures that she has looked forward to in life, yet she meets her death with courage. There is no cowardly whimpering or cringing in the face of death. She dies as she had lived, with honesty, with discipline and with courage.

Rinaldi

Lieutenant Henry's room-mate in the ambulance corps, Rinaldi is an Italian surgeon. Boisterously high-spirited, his spontaneous freedom of gesture tends to embarrass Henry. Although he is the one who first meets Catherine Barkley, later conversation with Henry demonstrates that she is not his type. Her mannered decorum contrasts with Rinaldi's usual ease in conveying his emotions. However, the war changes Rinaldi. He becomes a more skilled surgeon, but he is increasingly disoriented. His only satisfactions, besides his work, are drink and prostitutes. The continuous turmoil of war gradually crushes his former optimism and exuberance.

The Priest

In contrast to Rinaldi, the priest is supported by his beliefs. He is able to find, even in the events of the terrible war, the possibility for hope, if only in the self-understanding men find in defeat. He is continuously subjected to merciless jokes and satirical comments by fellow officers at the mess. At first, he finds it difficult to endure. But by the time of Henry's return from his leave, the priest has found the strength to ignore the attacks upon him. Henry feels for both

Rinaldi and the priest, but shares neither the former's devotion to duty nor the latter's sustaining faith.

Nevertheless, Henry admires the priest for the rigid, disciplined set of values by which he lives. In view of the fact that Henry himself is searching for a code, a set of values, he respects those whose values are solidified, even though he cannot accept the values themselves. In symbolic terms, the priest represents the cool, dry country of Abruzzi, an image that, to Henry, seems good and ordered and disciplined when compared to the disorder, lack of discipline and the ugliness found in the war. Henry will not reject a person because his views are different from his own. As can be seen in his unwillingness to "bait" the priest, Henry has a certain respect for this man and for the strength of his convictions, however incompatible they might be with his own.

Meaning

A Farewell to Arms can be regarded simply as the story of a man whose experiences of love and war lead to tragedy. But the novel is more than that. Hemingway has, with characteristic subtlety and skill, woven together a multiplicity of themes to form a work of art. In it we see the portrayal of a man who changes, who comes to an understanding of himself and the values by which he lives.

As in many of Hemingway's novels and short stories, we are shown the development of the protagonist as he learns to confront the ultimate (and often harsh) realities of life with courage and dignity. Whether in the context of the hunt (as in "The Short, Happy Life of Francis Macomber"), the bullfight (as in *The Sun Also Rises*) or, as in this case, the battlefield, the Hemingway man is initiated into the principles of the code hero. In doing so, he comes to understand the futility of clinging to those things in life which are essentially meaningless and, conversely, to accept that which is inescapably real.

In *A Farewell to Arms,* we see the development of the narrator and principle character, Frederic Henry, over the course of his involvement in World War I and his love affair with Catherine Barkley. At the beginning of the novel, it is apparent that Henry, while disillusioned by life, does not fully understand the horrors of war, nor does he comprehend the final reality of death. Henry has, presumably, lost some of the idealism that prompted him to volunteer for the army but, having only observed death from the somewhat limited perspective of an ambulance driver, he is still unable to fully understand the meaning of death. By contrast, Catherine is introduced as one who, having recently lost her fiancé to the war, possesses a clear insight into the irrevocable finality of death.

Catherine can be seen as a static character, against whom Henry's development can be measured. In a sense, she has already acquired the values of a code hero: she understands and accepts death and, as we learn from her conversation with Henry, she feels a keen sense of remorse because she and her fiancé had never consummated their love prior to his leaving for battle. Now that he will never return, Catherine sees the ultimate worthlessness of the conventional morality that prevented her from premarital sexual activity. Consequently, she has no qualms about sleeping with Henry, regarding it as merely a natural expression of her love for him. She resists Henry's suggestion that they get married, since she sees no meaning in the ceremony over and above the love they have for one another. Clearly, it is Catherine who has discarded the conventions of society. Henry, as yet untouched by death, still holds to the institution of Western civilization as a necessary order in life.

The theme of death in the novel is illustrated in the progressive stages through which Henry begins to understand it. The sense of relative safety that Henry felt at the beginning of the book is shattered when he is seriously wounded by a mortar shell. War and death take on a new meaning as Henry is made painfully aware of his own mortality. Later in the novel, during the disastrous retreat from Caporetto, Henry witnesses the purposeless death of a fellow ambulance driver who is shot by his own troops. Finally, when faced with the prospect of execution at the hands of the frenzied Italian military police, Henry rejects the absurdity of army discipline and makes his "farewell to arms."

Henry is unable to divorce himself completely from the bonds of traditional order. Even though he deserts the crumbling Italian army to save his own life, he is nevertheless unable to reconcile himself to the fact that he is not a traitor. Catherine, however, is not concerned, since patriotism and loyalty are, in her view, merely the bogus values adopted by others. The war is not "theirs"—the only reality is the love that exists for them as individuals. Unlike Henry, Catherine has succeeded in isolating herself from any sense of obligation to the conventions of society.

It is not until the end of the book that Henry finally assumes the values of the code hero. Catherine's death becomes the ultimate reality and, as he stares at the lifeless statue that had once been the woman he loved, Henry understands that death is inseparable from life and that rather than blindly accept the rules and conventions that society imposes on us, we must create our own codes and values.

Despite Henry's initial reluctance to adopt the values of the code hero, he does, nevertheless, exhibit a number of the mannerisms typical of the role. He is restless, preferring to stay awake at night and sleep during the day. Like many of Hemingway's heroes, he sees the combination of sleep and darkness as an obliteration of consciousness, a state in which a man is no longer a creature of will and action, but rather a passive, non-existent being. In the short story "A Clean, Well-Lighted Place," the hero does not sleep in the darkness, preferring instead to sleep with the light on. Similarly, Henry devotes his nights to drinking, carousing or making love. Catherine also conforms to this pattern, taking the night shift at the hospital so that she and Henry can make love.

Structure

The novel is divided into five books, each of which represents a distinct thematic segment of the work as a whole.

In the first book, Henry meets Catherine and is subsequently wounded in battle. The second book develops the love affair between Henry and Catherine, which blossoms during their time together at the hospital in Milan. The third book is devoted to the disasterous retreat from Caporetto, climaxing with Henry's desertion from the Italian army. The fourth deals with Henry's flight to Stresa and then to Switzerland with Catherine. The fifth book presents the couple's idyllic life in Switzerland, ending abruptly with Catherine's death during childbirth.

Taking the love affair and war as the two predominant plots in the novel, we can see the neatly balanced structure that Hemingway has created. Both love and war are introduced in the first book, preparing the reader for Henry's eventual farewell to war in the third book and to love in the fifth. Book II deals exclusively with love and this is balanced by the similar theme of Book IV. The third book develops the war plot and represents both the turning point for Frederic Henry (who makes his farewell to arms) and the central pivot in the structure of the novel. Using a more graphic analogy, the structure of *A Farewell to Arms* can be compared to a hill where Book III is its peak, Books II and IV are its slopes and where Book I and V represent the level ground on either side.

The symmetry of the novel is the most notable aspect of its structure. We have the "core" (Books II, III and IV) that consists alternately of the love and war plots. On one side of the core, we have Book I, where Henry is crippled by the war. On the other we have Book V, where he is crippled by love.

Style

Hemingway's style in *A Farewell to Arms* is essentially simple and straightforward, uncluttered by adjectives or the complexities of sentence structure which might detract from his description of action and fact. The reader is rarely provided with any narrative that characterizes the emotions or thoughts of the people in the novel. We are given only the essential ingredients, which must serve to inspire the emotions *in us*.

Hemingway takes great pains to avoid evoking a particular or intended response in the reader. He presents the facts in the most objective manner possible in order to convey the truth of the experience and, consequently, to inspire the most genuine emotions. Unlike many authors who direct the reader's attention through the use of main subordinate clauses or by the presentation of facts in a deliberate order, Hemingway strives for the simplest approach. In the first chapter of the novel, the sentences used are compound—simple sentences strung together with conjunctions like ''and'' or ''but.'' Facts and descriptions are presented in an almost random order, with no apparent preference given to any part.

The dialogue presented in the novel shares with the narrative a unique brand of simplicity. Although it has been argued that Hemingway's dialogue is stripped to the point of being artificial, it is nevertheless effective in the clarity of its expression. Hemingway does not use speech with the sole intention of making it realistic, but also with the purpose of revealing the character to the reader in the clearest, simplest way possible.

Hemingway rarely uses abstract words, nor does he employ adjectives or adverbs the meaning of which cannot be precisely defined. The author, like the hero in the novel, demonstrates a general distrust of rhetoric, slogans or empty phrases.

Finally, we may conclude our analysis of Hemingway's style by considering his own words on the subject:

> I do most of my work in my head. I never begin to write until my ideas are in order. Frequently I recite passages of dialogue as it is being written; the ear is a good censor. I never set down a sentence on paper until I have it so expressed that it will be clear to anyone.
>
> Yet I sometimes think that my style is suggestive rather than direct. The reader must often use his imagination or lose the most subtle part of my thoughts.

I take great pains with my work, pruning and revising with a tireless hand. I have the welfare of my creations very much at heart. I cut them with infinite care, and burnish them until they become brilliants. What many another writer would be content to leave in massive proportion, I polish into a tiny gem.

*Themes in *A Farewell to Arms*

I

Ernest Hemingway's first three important works were *In Our Time*, a collection of curiously related short stories; *The Sun Also Rises*, his first serious and successful novel; and *A Farewell to Arms*. All three deal with the same subject: the condition of man in a society upset by the violence of war. The short stories, while complete (almost idyllic) within themselves, take on an added dimension when viewed against the animal cruelty of the connecting war scenes. *The Sun Also Rises*, although set in the postwar period, is conditioned by the wartime disability of its principal figure, Jake Barnes. But the setting for *A Farewell to Arms* is the war itself, and the romance of Frederic Henry and Catherine Barkley, their attempt to escape the war and its resulting chaos, is a parable of twentieth-century man's disgust and disillusionment at the failure of civilization to achieve the ideals it had been promising throughout the nineteenth century. While the relation of one story to another in *In Our Time* is more or less arbitrary, while the meandering action of the ex-patriots' excursion into Spain in *The Sun Also Rises* is at most emblematic, the sequence of events in *A Farewell to Arms* is ordered and logical to an extreme which (outside of Henry James) is the exception in the American novel.

As a matter of fact, the physical form of *A Farewell to Arms* more nearly resembles the drama than it does the majority of American works of fiction. It is composed of five separate books, each composed of a series of scenes, and each scene broken into sections which might be likened to stage direction and dialogue. Thus, in section one we have the introduction of all major characters, the general war setting, and a statement of the problems involved; in section two the development of the romance between Frederic and Catherine; in section three, the retreat at Caporetto and the decision of Frederic to escape the chaos of war; in section four, the supposed escape, the rowing of Frederic and Catherine across the lake into Switzerland; and in section five, the hope of sanctuary which, through a reversal reminiscent again of the drama, comes to a climax in the ironic scene of Catherine's death while giving birth to their child.

*Editor's title. By Ray B. West, Jr. From "Ernest Hemingway: *A Farewell to Arms*," in The *Sewanee Review* 55 (Winter, 1945).

As Robert Penn Warren has pointed out (*Kenyon Review:* Winter, 1947), *A Farewell to Arms,* while not a religious book in the usual sense, depends upon a consciousness of the religious problems of our time. Its subject is the search for truth—for ethical standards to replace those which seemed impossible under the wartime conditions which it depicts. The use of the Christian religion is not, however, confined to the conventional uses of the ordinary religious novel, in which the characters are evaluated according to their acceptance or rejection of orthodox views. Rather, it is ironically implied, for instance, that Catherine, who is repeatedly portrayed as one with no orthodox religious sense, is really on the side of the priest, whose orthodoxy is beyond question. It is implied, too, that the priest's religious sensibility, like the sensibility of all of the participants in the novel's action, is heightened by the events of the war. After the difficult summer, during which Frederic was confined in the hospital, all of the men in his group have been softened. "Where are all the good old priest-baiters?" Rinaldi asks. "Do I have to bait this priest alone without support?" Frederic could see that the baiting which had gone on earlier did not touch the priest now. In talking with the priest he makes a distinction which is important to our interpretation of all the characters: even the priest is now not only technically a Christian, he is more like Our Lord. "It is," Frederic says, "in defeat that we become Christians."

On the other hand, it is not merely the humility of defeat, but the result of active participation (a first-hand acquaintance with the objective facts instead of the abstract theories of warfare) which makes all the difference. Outward forms divorced from action do not suffice, as when the soldier under Frederic refuses to believe that the Austrians were going to attack, because, as he said, "What has been done this summer cannot have been done in vain." Frederic thinks:

> I was always embarrassed by the words sacred, glorious, and sacrifice and the expression in vain. We had heard them, sometimes standing in the rain almost out of earshot, so that only the shouted words came through, and had read them, on proclamations that were slapped up by billposters over other proclamations, now for a long time, and I had seen nothing sacred, and the things that were glorious had no glory and the sacrifices were like the stockyards at Chicago if nothing was done with the meat except to bury

it. There were many words that you could not stand to hear
and finally only the names of places had dignity.

When the words became separated from the acts they were meant
to describe, then they meant nothing; the slaughter of war was less
than the slaughter of animals in the stockyard. The names of places
had dignity because the places still had some objective reality. Likewise, the acts of Rinaldi when he is practising his craft, of Dr.
Valentini (but not of the incompetent physicians), have dignity because they are done surely and skillfully—to some purpose. The
early stages of Frederic and Catherine's courtship were like moves
in a chess game or a game of bridge; later it became something
different, so different that even the outward form of marriage could
make no difference. Catherine asks: "What good would it do to
marry now? We're really married. I couldn't be any more married."
Even the war, when Frederic was no longer participating, "seemed
as far away as the football games of some one else's college." No
activity has meaning unless the participant is emotionally involved;
this is the real test, like the names of places. There is Christianity
and there are true Christians. There is incompetence and competence.
There is marriage and there is true love. In a story in *In Our Time*,
we have the picture of a bullfighter who is defeated and derided by
the crowd, but he is really "The Undefeated" (the title of the story),
because he is only outwardly not inwardly defeated. As we have
seen, in "The Short Happy Life" even death does not defeat Francis
Macomber, for it is in death that he triumphs.

But what is the real distinction between the failures—the defeated—and the *genuine* men and women in the novel—what critics
have come to call "the initiated"? Rinaldi (who is one of them) says
to Frederic at the time when Frederic returns to the front: "You
puncture men when I become a great Italian thinker. But I know
many things I can't say." Frederic, when he is talking to the priest
after his return from the hospital, says: "I never think and yet when
I begin to talk I say the things I have found out in my mind without
thinking." There are times when Catherine "feels" immoral, but
most of the time she "feels" that her love is sanctified. The peasants
and the defeated soldiers have wisdom because they are not misled
by the empty forms. Hemingway seems to be saying, like William
Wordsworth, that such men are by circumstance closer to reality—
and thus to wisdom. In the book which followed *A Farewell to
Arms—Death in the Afternoon*—Hemingway says, "Morals are what

you feel good after." Brett Ashley in *The Sun Also Rises* decides to give up a love affair because it makes her *feel* good "deciding not to be a bitch." The test of morals is the unadulterated sensibility—the sensibility not misled by the empty forms of patriotism, religion, and love: the sensibility of Rinaldi when he does not attempt to be a great Italian thinker; the sensibility of Dr. Valentini, who knows at once what is to be done and does it without quibble and consultation; the sensibility of the peasants; the sensibility of Catherine, who learns from her love for Frederic that it is all right, who says: "Everything we do seems so innocent and simple. I can't believe we do anything wrong." Even the sensibility of Frederic, which is the developing moral sense of the novel, is superior to Rinaldi's because it has greater scope—the surgeon is happy only when he is working. "I know more than you," Rinaldi says, and Frederic agrees with him. "But you will have a better time. Even with remorse you will have a better time."

It is this limiting quality in Frederic's character which points to the principal problem of the novel. Rinaldi calls it remorse. Frederic cannot completely escape the forms of his early training, though he makes a systematic progress throughout the book. Before he was wounded he had attempted to accept Catherine's philosophy that death is the end, but his experience seemed to prove otherwise, for in her antireligious position Catherine is as orthodox as the priest. Frederic says: "I felt myself rush bodily out of myself and out and out and out and all the time bodily in the wind. I went out swiftly, all of myself, and I knew I was dead and that it had all been a mistake to think you just died." This is Hemingway's mysticism which triumphed in *For Whom the Bell Tolls* and which was at its lowest ebb in his curious little essay "A Natural History of the Dead." Frederic does not love God, but he is afraid of him in the night sometimes. Because he does not "belong," he and Catherine cannot find sanctuary in the church the evening they are waiting for the train, though an Italian couple does. Yet Frederic is much more anxious about the absence of the marriage ceremony than Catherine, and when the child is born dead he is disturbed because it had not been baptized. The limitations of Frederic's religious sensibility (a symbol for the religious sensibility of our time) are depicted in two scenes, the first in his failure to visit the home of the priest at Abruzzi, where "You would like the people and though it is cold it is clear and dry"; the second is the incident at the church:

There were streetcar tracks and beyond them was the cathedral. It was white and wet in the mist. We crossed the tram tracks. On our left were the shops, their windows lighted, and the entrance to the galleria. There was a fog in the square and when we came close to the front of the cathedral it was very big and the stone was wet.

"Would you like to go in?"

"No," Catherine said. We walked along. There was a soldier standing with his girl in the shadow of one of the stone buttresses ahead of us and we passed them. They were standing tight up against the stone and he had put his cape around her.

"They're like us," I said.

"Nobody is like us," Catherine said. She did not mean it happily.

"I wish they had some place to go."

"It mightn't do them any good."

"I don't know. Everybody ought to have some place to go."

"They have the cathedral," Catherine said. (Chapter 23)

Catherine and Frederic have a hotel room (the "lost generation"), while the Italian soldier and his girl have the cathedral; the priest has his cold, clear, dry country; the atheists have their houses of prostitution. The priest's country appeals to Frederic, and he is sorry he did not visit it while he was on leave:

I had wanted to go to Abruzzi. I had gone to no place where the roads were frozen and hard as iron, where it was clear cold and dry and the snow was dry and powdery and hare-tracks in the snow and the peasants took off their hats and called you Lord and there was good hunting. I had gone to no such place but to the smoke of cafés and nights when the room whirled and you needed to look at the wall to make it stop, nights in bed, drunk, when you know that that was all there was, and the strange excitement of waking and not knowing who it was with you, and the world all unreal in the dark and so exciting that you must resume again unknowing and not caring in the night, sure that this was all and all and all and not caring. (Chapter 3)

Here is the symbol of Frederic's predicament, a key passage, since it represents the religious contrast. The priest's religion is his clear, cold country; Catherine's religion is her love, which, as Count Greffi says, "is a religious feeling," or, as Catherine tells Frederic: "You're my religion. You're all I've got." Frederic is the modern hero, lost between two worlds, the world of tradition and certainty which he cannot wholly relinquish, and the exciting but uncertain world of the twentieth century, where you only occasionally find something substantial to look at to make everything stop whirling, where you live for the moment, giving yourself up to sensations, for it is through the senses that you discover truth: the strong man giving equal odds to his weaker opponent, the boxer, the hunter, the bull-fighter, the soldier, and the lover; the strong man aware that the only order in the universe is that which he himself can supply, but aware, too, that such order is transitory, that perhaps the highest possible values consist in pure sensation which seeks out new order and a stoicism which transcends physical defeat.

II

At the beginning Frederic wavers between reason and sensibility, between formal religion and "true" Christianity, between the empty forms of love and true love. He has been thrust into a world of violent action in which choice is eventually to become necessary. An English critic has called Frederic "a curiously passive hero," but this is true only in the sense that Thomas Mann's Herr Friedemann was passive. The Hemingway hero is, theoretically, passive, because he is allied to nature through his unreason, but his particular dilemma usually has all the appearances of active seeking.

Frederic's relationship to Catherine in Book I is like a game of bridge where you pretend to be playing for stakes, but do not know what the stakes are. At the end of the section Frederic is wounded, but not seriously. It is the first hint that what he had called "the picturesque front" was capable of becoming something else. It is a foreshadowing of the retreat at Caporetto.

In Book II the action takes place in the American hospital at Milan, and almost at once we know that the formal relationship (love like a bridge game or a game of chess) has ended. Frederic thinks:

God knows I had not wanted to fall in love with her.
I had not wanted to fall in love with any one. But God

knows I had and I lay on the bed in the room of the hospital in Milan and all sorts of things went through my head but I felt wonderful . . . (Chapter 14)

We are introduced to the incompetent doctors and to the professional patriots like Ettore. Frederic, although he cannot reject Ettore as completely as Catherine, does reject his own decoration, because he knows that he is not a hero. The silver medal repeats the pattern of the empty form. A new action is suggested in this book by Catherine's fear of death. She is afraid of the rain, she says, and when pressed by Frederic for an explanation, admits that it is because she sometimes sees herself dead in it. Frederic is unbelieving. "And sometimes I see you dead in it," she adds. "That's more likely," Frederic says. "No it's not, darling. Because I can keep you safe. I know I can. But nobody can help themselves." Here is one of the secrets of the passivity of Hemingway's characters. Later in the section, when Catherine admits that she is going to have a baby:

"You aren't angry are you, darling?"
"No."
"And you don't feel trapped?"
"Maybe a little. But not by you."
"I didn't mean by me. You must be stupid. I meant trapped at all."
"You always feel trapped biologically." (Chapter 21)

"Biologically," in the Hemingway world, covers just about everything; there is nothing you can do about life but accept it with stoicism. This is an anticipation of the final scenes in the novel, but Frederic, fortunately, did not realize how final the trap was:

Poor, poor dear Cat. And this was the price you paid for sleeping together. This was the end of the trap. This was what people got for loving each other. (Chapter 41)

In this book, however, the threat is taken only seriously enough to provoke discussion of death and the conditions of man's dying. Frederic has quoted the line, "The coward dies a thousand deaths, the brave but one"; Catherine replies: "The brave dies perhaps two thousand deaths if he's intelligent. He simply doesn't mention them."

There is an indication that Frederic is very little different from Catherine in his fear of death. They are in a café and it is raining. He quotes Andrew Marvell: "But at my back I always hear/Time's wingéd chariot hurrying near." He wants to talk facts. Where will the baby be born? Catherine refuses stoically) to discuss it. "Then don't worry, darling," she tells him. "You were fine until now and now you're worrying."

The tone of this section suggests death, but the reader does not know, any more than do Catherine and Frederic, whose death it is to be. Frederic returns to the front, where there are rumors of a new attack by the Austrians. Catherine awaits the time when she will have her baby. Both are, in a sense, trapped—trapped by the war, by their love, and (though they are unaware of it) by death.

At the very beginning of Book III we are introduced to the town of Caporetto. Frederic "remembered it as a little white town with a campanile in a valley. It was a clean little town and there was a fine fountain in the square." This is where the summer fighting has ended. One of Hemingway's most constant symbols of the goal which his heroes seek is—to utilize the title of one of his stories—a "Clean, Well-Lighted Place." War has undoubtedly destroyed the "clean little town," but this is just an additional indication of war's ugliness. Caporetto is the point where the Austrians succeed in breaking through and turning Frederic's "picturesque front" into a machine of destruction. There are only isolated examples of decency and order in the retreat; the whole atmosphere is one of anarchy and confusion.

Malcolm Cowley has likened Frederic's plunge into the river to escape execution as a baptism—a symbol of Frederic's entering the world of the initiated, but this is true only in so far as it refers to his decision (his rebirth) concerning the war. The chapters preceding, where Frederic returns to the front and meets his old comrades, indicate both how much he had learned through his stay at the hospital (the baptism of love) and how much the members of his company have learned through the difficult fighting of the summer (their baptism of fire), but the final consecration does not come until later when Frederic is confronted by love and death at the same time. The retreat does, however, represent a major phase in his initiation. Frederic is in the position of the fat gray-haired little lieutenant-colonel whom the carabinieri were questioning at the bridge.

> The questioners had all the efficiency, coldness and command of themselves of Italians who are firing and are not being fired on.

"Your brigade?"

He told them.

"Regiment?"

He told them.

"Why are you not with your regiment?"

He told them.

"Do you not know that an officer should be with his troops?"

He did.

That was all. Another officer spoke.

"It is you and such as you that have let the barbarians onto the sacred soil of the fatherland."

"I beg your pardon," said the lieutenant-colonel.

"It is because of treachery such as yours that we have lost the fruits of victory."

"Have you ever been in a retreat?" the lieutenant-colonel asked. (Chapter 30)

The military police are firing but are not being fired on. They are like religious persons who have never been tempted, condemning the sinner who has succumbed; the police have the hollow shell of patriotism, using such phrases as "the sacred soil of the fatherland" and "the fruits of victory," but it is punctured by the lieutenant-colonel's simple question: "Have you ever been in a retreat?" The carabiniere's brave words have no relation to the reality of the situation, while the condemned man's question goes right to the heart of it. Frederic rationalizes his own situation as follows:

You had lost your cars and your men as a floorwalker loses the stock of his department in a fire. There was, however, no insurance. You were out of it now. You had no more obligation. If they shot the floorwalker after a fire in the department store because they spoke with an accent they had always had, then certainly the floorwalkers would not be expected to return when the store opened again for business. They might seek other employment; if there was any other employment and the police did not get them.

Anger was washed away in the river along with any obligation. Although that ceased when the carabiniere put his hands on my collar. I would like to have had the uniform off *although I did not care much about the outward forms*

> [our italics] I had taken off the stars, but that was for convenience. It was no point of honor. I was not against them. I was through. I wished them all the luck. There were the good ones, and the brave ones, and the calm ones, and the sensible ones, and they deserved it. But it was not my show any more and I wished this bloody train would get to Mestre and I would eat and stop thinking. I would have to stop. (Chapter 32)

The fighter obeys the rules until they are suspended or no longer enforced; then he gets out of the ring (cf. Margot Macomber in "The Short Happy Life"). With the retreat at Caporetto, the Austrian front ceased to be "the picturesque front"; it is no longer subject to the traditional rules of "honorable" warfare. Frederic, too, for the time being ceases to be the "curiously passive hero." He cannot escape the war until he escapes from Italy with Catherine, and to escape is to struggle.

Yet according to the standards of Frederic Henry's world, such a decision is in itself dangerous. His reasoning is too pat, his assurance too great. The determination to struggle becomes a kind of "tragic flaw"—a brash modern pride which tempts fate as the occupants of Stephen Crane's little boat tempt the seven mad gods of the sea. Hemingway hints at this in the beginning of Book IV. In the hotel at Stresa, where Frederic went to find Catherine, the barman asks him questions about the war.

> "Don't talk about the war," I said. The war was a long way off. Maybe there wasn't any war. There was no war here. Then I realized it was over for me. But I did not have the feeling that it was really over. I had the feeling of a boy who thinks of what is happening at a certain hour at the schoolhouse from which he has played truant. (Chapter 34)

The war is not over. Even after the successful effort to leave Italy and enter Switzerland, the war (which is really a symbol for the chaos of nature—the biological trap) catches up with Frederic and Catherine. It is significant that Frederic's reason tells him he can escape—that he *has* escaped; his sensibility suggests that he is only playing truant. Frederic felt like a masquerader in his civilian clothes. That is to say, in the modern sense, all happiness is a form of truancy. The months in Switzerland were idyllic. Even the snow came late, almost as though Frederic had ordered nature's cooperation.

The trap is sprung in Book V. Catherine's confinement is difficult, and the birth when it does come is finally performed through a Caesarean operation. The child is born dead. Catherine herself dies soon afterward. Yet, though it is Catherine who dies, *A Farewell to Arms* is not her tragedy. Unlike Francis Macomber and unlike Manuelo in "The Undefeated," she does not *become* admirable in her dying; she *remains* admirable according to the rules of decorum which Hemingway has set up:

> The nurse opened the door and motioned with her finger for me to come. I followed her into the room. Catherine did not look up when I came in. I went over to the side of the bed. The doctor was standing by the bed on the opposite side. Catherine looked at me and smiled. I bent down over the bed and started to cry.
>
> "Poor darling," Catherine said very softly. She looked gray.
>
> "You're all right, Cat," I said. "You're going to be all right."
>
> "I'm going to die," she said; then waited and said, "I hate it."
>
> I took her hand.
>
> "Don't touch me," she said. I let go of her hand. She smiled. "Poor darling. You touch me all you want."
>
> "You'll be all right, Cat. I know you'll be all right."
>
> "I meant to write you a letter to have if anything happened, but I didn't do it."
>
> "Do you want me to get a priest or any one to come and see you?"
>
> "Just you," she said. Then a little later, "I'm not afraid. I just hate it." (Chapter 41)

Catherine had had the perception of death early, but it had come to Frederic only since learning of the doctor's fears. During the operation he thought she was dead: "Her face was gray." Catherine knows intuitively that she is going to die. Frederic senses it, but his reason will not allow him to accept it, as she does, as "just a dirty trick."

I knew she was going to die and I prayed that she would not. Don't let her die. Oh, God, please don't let her die. I'll do anything for you if you won't let her die. Please, please, please, dear God, don't let her die. Dear God, don't let her die. Please, please, please don't let her die. God please make her not die. I'll do anything you say if you don't let her die. You took the baby but don't let her die. That was all right, but don't let her die. Please, please, dear God, don't let her die. (Chapter 41)

Frederic's hope that he could prevent her from dying is as illusory as his belief that he could escape the war by signing a separate peace. In a sense, Frederic is a depiction of the narrator's figure in ''The Open Boat,'' who, when he realizes that there is no tangible thing to hoot, feels the desire to confront a personification and indulge in pleas. It isn't until he has accepted the terrible reality of Catherine's death that he is truly initiated: ''It was like saying good-by to a statue.'' This is the biological trap—sprung. Catherine has been right from the beginning. Early in the novel, in speaking of her English lover who was killed in France, she says: ''I thought perhaps he couldn't stand it and then of course he was killed and that was the end of it.'' ''I don't know,'' Frederic said. ''Oh, yes,'' Catherine emphasizes. ''That's the end of it.''

These are the limits, then, as circumscribed by nature: death is the end of life. After death there is only the lifeless statue. It was this conclusion (or something like it) which caused Gertrude Stein to say of Ernest Hemingway that he belonged to the ''lost generation,'' lost because the comfortable morality of the nineteenth century had been denied them after 1914. Frederic Henry attempts to believe in the validity of warfare, but even the peasant soldiers under him know better. When he puts his trust in religion or in his love for Catherine he is also defeated. He reasons it out as follows:

That was what you did. You died. You did not know what it was about. You never had time to learn. They threw you in and told you the rules and the first time they caught you off base they killed you. (Chapter 41)

In ''The Short Happy Life of Francis Macomber'' the emphasis was upon man's final victory over death. That view is represented here in the stoical death of Catherine, but the emphasis is upon futility. In a striking image which represents the key scene in the novel, we have Frederic thinking about an experience he has had:

> Once in camp I put a log on top of the fire and it was full of ants. As it commenced to burn, the ants swarmed out and went first toward the centre where the fire was; then turned back and ran toward the end. When there was enough on the end they fell off into the fire. Some got out, their bodies burnt and flattened, and went off not knowing where they were going. But most of them went toward the fire and back toward the end and swarmed on the cool end and finally fell off into the fire. I remember thinking at the time that it was the end of the world and a splendid chance to be a messiah and lift the log off the fire and throw it out where the ants could get off onto the ground. But I did not do anything but throw a tin cup of water on the log, so that I would have the cup empty to put whiskey in before I added water to it. I think the cup of water on the burning log only steamed the ants. (Chapter 41)

The relationship of this parable to Catherine's predicament is unmistakable. For her there is likewise no messiah to come to the rescue. Death is the end of it, and the only value in death is man's knowledge of it. In Ernest Heminway's novels, those who live well die like heroes. They are the initiated. But the initiation of Frederic Henry comes gradually. He learns about war, love, and finally death. Catherine's death is the final stage in his initiation.

III

If this conclusion is true, we might ask: "Why the title: *A Farewell to Arms*"? The title suggests in its obvious implications that the author saw his subject concerned primarily with the war. In that case, we might say either that we are wrong in our conclusions or that the author was wrong in his selection of title. This raises the question of Ernest Hemingway's method—his style. Hemingway's sensibility, when it is functioning at its highest point, has always worked upon an immediate objective level which translates ideas into terms of concrete things: life as a baseball game where each error is punished by death or compared to the struggle of ants on a burning log, the comparison of a hero's death with the slaughter of animals at a stockyard. In each case we are aware of the double implication, the idea and the image; and the emotional force of the idea is intensified by the shock supplied by the image. This is the more complicated form of Hemingway's noted "understatement." At the time of Catherine's operation, while the doctor has gone to make his preparations, Frederic is left to administer the anesthesia. He has been told that the correct amount would register upon the dial at number 2, but when Catherine is in extreme pain, he says, "I turned the dial to three and then four. I wished the doctor would come back. I was afraid of the numbers above two." The statement "I wished the doctor would come back" is understatement. The use of the machine-image suggests Catherine's immediate danger. Another author might have examined in great detail both Catherine's illness and the emotion which Frederic was experiencing at that time; but from the simple, quiet statement, reinforced by the dial registering the numbers above two, we get the full force of Frederic's terror in a few strokes.

That Hemingway was aware of this quality is evidenced by the statement which he once made that what he was attempting to get was a "fifth dimension" in his prose; not the ordinary dimensions of exposition and description, but the full quality of the emotional experience. This is not an unusual characteristic of a work of art; it is merely Ernest Hemingway's means of explaining his own intention; but it suggests the caution a reader should exercise in taking the author's words or sentences at their most obvious level of meaning. Perhaps this is true also of the title, *A Farewell to Arms*. Someone has suggested somewhere that the "Arms" referred not to the war, but to the arms of Catherine; thus suggesting that what the novel was about, really, was Frederic's loss of his love. This is as limited an interpretation as that which sees the novel as only a "war novel." A more valid interpretation would see the title as completely ironic. Frederic has attempted to escape from the obligations which life imposes. He did not wish to fall in love, but he did. He attempted to escape the war, but he felt like a schoolboy who was playing truant. His life with Catherine in Switzerland and the life which they anticipated after the war were relatively devoid of conflict. Catherine and Frederic had said farewell to the life of action and struggle, but ironically their greatest test—the attempt to save the life of Catherine—came at the very moment when they seemed to have achieved successful escape.

What the novel says, finally, is that you cannot escape the obligations of action—you cannot say "farewell to arms"; you cannot sign a separate peace. You can only learn to live with life, to tolerate it as "the initiated" learn to tolerate it.

Selected Criticisms

. . . In *A Farewell to Arms,* the rain becomes a conscious symbol of disaster. "Things went very badly," the hero tells us in the first chapter. "At the start of the winter came the permanent rain and with the rain came the cholera." Catherine Barkley is afraid of the rain because, she says, "sometimes I see me dead in it." Rain falls all during the retreat from Caporetto; it falls while Catherine is trying to have her baby in a Swiss hospital; and it is still falling when she dies and when Frederic pushes the nurses out of the room to be alone with her. "It wasn't any good," he says. "It was like saying goodbye to a statue. After a while I went out and left the hospital and walked back to the hotel in the rain." On the other hand, it is snow that is used as a symbol of death in "The Snows of Kilomanjaro" (along with other death symbols, like vultures, hyenas, and soaring in an imaginary airplane). And possibly snow has the same value in *For Whom the Bell Tolls,* where a spring snowfall adds to the danger of Robert Jordan's mission and indirectly causes his death.

Malcolm Cowley, "Introduction" to *The Portable Hemingway.* Viking Press, 1944.

One thing is noticeable immediately: as in virtually all of Hemingway, anything that can possibly be construed to operate symbolically does no violence whatsoever to the naturalism (or realism) of the story on the primary level. Nothing could be a more natural—or more traditional—symbol of purity, of escape from the commonplace, in short of elevation, than mountains. If thousands of people have read the passages in *A Farewell to Arms* which associate the mountains "with dry-cold weather; with peace and quiet; with love, dignity, health, happiness and the good life" without taking them to be "symbolic" it is presumably because these associations are almost second nature for all of us. Certainly this seems to be true of Frederic Henry: it is most doubtful that in the course of the novel he is ever to be imagined as consciously regarding the mountains as a symbol. This of course does not prove that Hemingway did not regard them as such, or that the full understanding of this novel as an art structure does not perhaps require the symbolic equation, *mountain* equals *life and home.* It does, however, point differentially to another type of symbolism, where the character in question is shown to be clearly aware of the trope, as when Catherine Barkley

93

says she hates rain because "sometimes I see me dead in it," or when Frederic Henry says of his plunge into the Tagliamento, "Anger was washed away in the river along with any obligation."[5]

E. M. Halliday, *American Literature* 27 (1956).

While is is true that Catherine's death concludes the novel, her death is really only the end of a beginning as far as Frederic Henry is concerned; he is now ready to reflect on his recent experiences and to present them to the reader, and he is a very sophisticated narrator. He is not merely recounting events in an objective way. (If he were, the advantage of the first-person over a third-person point of view would be questionable.) Like many of the protagonists of the short stories and like Jake Barnes, another first-person narrator, Henry has undergone an initiatory and learning experience that he is now ready to interpret. The wonderful sense of immediacy that Henry can convey in this most brilliantly written of Hemingway's novels should not mislead the reader into thinking that the events transpire and are immediately recorded in a diary or epistolary form.

Robert W. Lewis, Jr. *Hemingway on Love*. University of Texas Press, 1965.

The harsh note of suppressed grief on which this story closes expresses the fatalistic stoicism which arises in the young American out of his inherent inner passivity as it is affected by his sense of futility and of loss. At such an intensity of suffering there are usually only two courses open to the human heart, a receptive softening or a cynical hardening. But we already know that a desperate, bitter hardness is a characteristic of Hemingway's work as a whole.

A survey of the ground covered by the greater part of Hemingway's writing shows it to be that indicated in the first part of this essay—the delineation of an eviscerated, chaotic world of futility and boredom lit up with flashes of violent action, where life is brought into a sensational vividness only by contrast with the nullity of death. The bulk of Hemingway's writing expresses consciously an outlook on life which is negative to the point of nihilism.

D. S. Savage, *The Withered Branch*. Eyre and Spottiswoode, 1950.

But the darkness of Catherine's death is a cloud spread by the author as a disguise for pulling off a *deus ex machina* to save his hero from the existential hell of a complicated life. Henry's philippic against the impersonal "they" that kills you—that killed Aymo gratuitously, that gave Rinaldi the syphilis, and that now is killing Catherine—is fine rhetoric and perhaps much in place for a universe without God in our time, but it is the author himself who is guilty of Catherine's death because of his fondness for the hero, and who makes a scapegoat of the world. The Henry who walks off into the rainy night at the end of *A Farewell to Arms* is like the Orestes who exists with the Furies in *Les Mouches*—he is alone, tormented, but very much alive in an existential sense.

Several critics have noted the recurrence of rain (or other forms of precipitation) in Hemingway's fiction, and especially in *A Farewell to Arms,* as a harbinger of disaster. Since it *is* connected with death, they generally agree that this function is diametrically opposite that of the precipitation symbol in the wasteland world of T. S. Eliot. But I believe that the rain is a symbol of fertility in Hemingway, too, though in a slightly different sense than in Eliot. To Hemingway death means rebirth for the existentialist hero in its presence, and therefore the rain, as an omen of death, at the same time predicts rebirth. The precipitation-death-rebirth combination is especially pertinent to the recurrent use of rain in *A Farewell to Arms* and of snow in *For Whom the Bell Tolls*; and a case might even be made for a theory that old Santiago, who is an existentialist in the grand style ("He was too simple to wonder when he had attained humility"), is an authentic individual because he is an old man *of the sea,* which is both a perennial reminder of man's finitude and a primordial womb symbol.

John Killinger, *Hemingway and the Dead Gods*. University of Kentucky Press, 1960.

Frederic Henry begins, particularly in his relation to women and love, from a completely self-centered position. On his leave early in the novel, Henry goes to the city and immerses himself completely in self-satisfaction. Later, when he meets Catherine, he looks upon her simply as an objective in a game of chess, another avenue to self-satisfaction. As I have pointed out, initially he cares very little for her emotional well-being or the fact that she has been driven emotionally off balance by her previous misfortunes. After Henry's wounding, he still does not love. The prescription for love offered by the priest (in terms of Christian love) remains unapprehended by him. When Catherine shows up at the American hospital in Milan, he sees her differently through this demonstration of devotion to him, and feels that he loves her. But it remains for Catherine to teach Henry what love really means; the period in the hospital becomes a period of introduction. . . . Catherine's emphasis here is on the love given in the act; Henry's emphasis is on the pleasure received and a concern for the continuation of it. For Hemingway, sex is an essential ingredient in the love between man and woman, and the continuation of Catherine and Henry's sexual relationship throughout the summer is the medium by which true regard for the other person is reached. Sex, too, is essentially an anti-sentimental ingredient of love. A full and honest giving and receiving of pleasure from the other partner contradicts those self-directed emotions of longing and self-pity which are central to love as sentimentality.

Jackson Benson, *The Writer's Art of Self-Defense*. University of Minnesota Press, 1969.

The most obvious connection between love and war here is that each makes for a part of the education of the hero. It is not war, however, which destroys Frederic Henry and his sweetheart. War is merely the situation in which their star-crossed love exists. the war serves as a gigantic metaphor of the indifference and cruelty of the universe. We might say that Hemingway is putting as a question what for Matthew Arnold was an assertion sixty years before: "Ah, love, let us be true to one another"; for the world is but "a darkling plain . . . /Where ignorant armies clash by night." In *A Farewell to Arms* Hemingway asks: is there any real value in lovers' being true to one another in such a world? Toward understanding Hemingway's answer, I suggest that we look closely at this love affair. To trace its development to its final destruction may lead us toward the center of Hemingway's vision of life.

R. B. Hovey, *Hemingway: The Inward Terrain*. University of Washington Press, 1968.

Neither in *Romeo and Juliet* nor in *A Farewell to Arms* is the catastrophe a direct and logical result of the immoral social situation. Catherine's bodily structure, which precludes a normal delivery for her baby, is an unfortunate biological accident. The death of Shakespeare's lovers is also precipitated by an accident—the detention of the message-bearing friar. The student of esthetics, recognizing another kind of logic in art than that of mathematical cause-and-effect, may however conclude that Catherine's death, like that of Juliet, shows a kind of artistic inevitability. Except by a large indirection, the war does not kill Catherine any more than the Veronese feud kills Juliet. But in the emotional experience of the novel, Catherine's dying is directly associated and interwoven with the whole tragic pattern of fatigue and suffering, loneliness, defeat and doom, of which the war is itself the broad social manifestation. And one might make a similar argument about *Romeo and Juliet*.

Carlos Baker, *Hemingway: The Writer as Artist*. Princeton University Press, 1963.

. . . In *A Farewell to Arms* it is society as a whole that is rejected, social responsibility, social concern. Lieutenant Henry is in the War, but his attitude toward it is purely that of a spectator, refusing to be involved. He is leading a private life as an isolated individual. Even personal relations, of any depth or intimacy, he avoids; he drinks with the officers and talks with the priest and visits the officers' brothel, but all contacts he keeps, deliberately, on a superficial level. He has rejected the world.

Such an attitude is possible only to a sensitive and reflective person. Henry is no naïve barbarian. He was studying architecture in Italy when the War began; he makes ironical remarks about sculptures and bronzes; his reflections and conversation contain allusions to Samuel Johnson, Saint Paul, Andrew Marvell, and Sir Thomas Wyatt. His flight from responsibility is the ultimate of the flight that Jake and Brett and Mike were trying to effect with drink and bullfights and sex. He is evading responsibility and emotion, taking refuge in simple primary sensations. Successfully, so far as the War is concerned. "I was always embarrassed by the words sacred, glorious and sacrifice and the expression in vain. . . . Abstract words, such as glory, honor, courage, or hallow were obscene beside the concrete names of villages, the number of roads, the names of rivers, the numbers of regiments and the dates."

It is hardly possible to miss the intensity here trying to masquerade as a hardboiled indifference, endeavoring to shore itself against the immeasurable cruelty of things and the callous glibness of words. Even more than Jake, Henry is immuring himself in an ivory tower of trying not to feel. But an indifference preserved in the face of such underlying emotion is precariously held. It breaks down upon his meeting with Catherine Barkley.

"God knows I had not wanted to fall in love with her. I had not wanted to fall in love with any one." Emotion has found an entering wedge, although Henry tries even now to draw a circle enclosing themselves alone. The world without is the enemy. "Because there's only us two and in the world there's all the rest of them," Catherine says. "If anything comes between us we're gone and they have us." Henry deserts, he escapes to Switzerland with Catherine. He no longer even reads about the fighting. "I was going to forget the war. I had made a separate peace." (So the dying boy in one of the interchapters of *In Our Time* whispers to his fatally wounded comrade, "You and me, we've made a separate peace.") But momentarily Hemingway tries to ignore the implication that the only separate peace is in death. He will solve the problem of dealing with the world by taking refuge in individualism and isolated personal relationships and sensations. He too will make a separate peace.

But the separate peace soon turns out to be impossible. Hemingway's honesty and understanding will not allow him to pretend it is successful. Catherine undergoes a prolonged and painful childbirth, and ultimately she dies. "You did not know what it was all about. You never had time to learn. They threw you in and told you the rules and the first time they caught you off base they killed you." In the end, then, one could not be a candle-holder and look on. Life caught you up, willy-nilly, by your instincts, by your sensations, by your emotions, caught you in a trap; and the better you were the harder it dealt with you. "If people bring so much courage to the world the world has to kill them to break them, so of course it kills them. . . . It kills the very good and the very gentle and the very grave impartially. If you are none of these you can be sure it will kill you too but there will be no special hurry."

Such is the result of trying to reject society and reject responsibility. It seemed to lead back with intensified bitterness to the vision of cosmic cruelty underlying *In Our Time*. Life was only an endless abrasion and destruction, even more harsh to the intelligent and the good than to all the others. To them it brings "only the remorseless devaluation of nature . . . which bears away of our great hopes, emotions, and ambitions only a few and soon disintegrating trifles." The end of the road was blank disheartenment, despair for life and civilization and mankind.

Edgar Johnson, *The Sewanee Review* 48 (1940).

Suggested Study Topics

The ability to complete the following assignments will give the reader deeper insight into the significance of *A Farewell to Arms* as a literary work. It is suggested that the reader write out these assignments and discuss them with his instructor or fellow classmates.

1. Hemingway said that modern American writing all stems from one book, Mark Twain's *Huckleberry Finn*. By direct reference to that book, show the similarity of styles and quality of experience between *A Farewell to Arms* and Twain's book, paying special attention to the "myth of escape" in *Huckleberry Finn,* and the violence that Huck meets.

2. "All he wanted, he said, was to know how to live. Later he said that all he wanted was to write well. Any discrepancy which might appear to exist between the two statements is illusory. Learning to write well was a way of learning defense." (Philip Young, *Ernest Hemingway*, p. 179). What is the implied relationship in this comment between Hemingway's ethics and his aesthetics? Explain.

3. Point out the significant similarities and contrasts between Doctor Rinaldi and the priest. What is the author's attitude toward these two characters?

4. Critics have pointed out very interesting technical similarities in the quality of some of the diction in Stendhal's *The Red and The Black* to some of Hemingway's most typical prose. Since Stendhal's novel is one of the first "realistic" pieces of long fiction, a comparison would be helpful.

5. F. Scott Fitzgerald was working on *The Great Gatsby* and his stories at about the same time as Hemingway's early career. The temperamental differences between the two men are instructive. In what way would you describe these differences?

6. A great deal has been made of Hemingway's "poetic" sensibility. Find the passages in *A Farewell to Arms* that seem most "poetic" to you and attempt an analysis of the particular aspects of his prose that create this impression. To what concept of poetry is this achievement related?

7. If Frederic Henry and Catherine Barkley had been allowed to have their child, and a certain continuity in their relationship, how do you see their future? In attempting an

analysis be careful to stick close to those attributes of temperament that the novel disclosed. By using relevant passages from the novel, try to justify your predictions.

8. What is the attitude towards war in *A Farewell to Arms*? Is this attitude relevant to the contemporary world? Is it consistent with your own ideas about war? Have the modern means of waging war, or potential wars, changed the validity of the concepts underlying *A Farewell to Arms*?

9. Is this novel a great book? Whatever your answer, it is essential that you methodically categorize those aspects of any novel that would permit you to use such a term as "great." Make up a short list of American and European novels that you consider to be in the same class as *A Farewell to Arms*.

10. Essentially, do you see this novel as an escape from violence and from evil, or does it appear to you that the fundamental accent of *A Farewell to Arms* may be taken to be the life-loving forces that bring the two together? Or is it something more complex than either answer by itself?

Bibliography

Aldridge, John W. *After the Lost Generation*. New York: Noonday Press, 1958.

Arnold, Lloyd R. *High on the Wild with Hemingway*. Caldwell, Idaho: Caxton, 1968.

Atkins, John. *The Art of Ernest Hemingway: His Work and Personality*. London: Spring Books, Inc., 1952.

Baker, Carlos. *Hemingway: the Writer as Artist*. Princeton: Princeton University Press, 1952.

Baker, Sheridan. *Ernest Hemingway: Introduction and Interpretation*. New York: Barnes & Noble, Inc., 1967.

Benson, Jackson J. *Hemingway: The Writer's Art of Self-Defense*. Minnepolis: University of Minnesota Press, 1969.

Burgum, Edwin Berry. "Ernest Hemingway and the Psychology of the Lost Generation," in his *The Novel and the World's Dilemma*. New York: Oxford University Press, 1947.

Cowley, Malcolm. "Hemingway and the Hero." *New Republic*, III. Dec., 1944.

Fenton, Charles A. *The Apprenticeship of Ernest Hemingway*. New York: Farrar, Straus & Young, Inc., 1952.

Hotchner, A. E. *Papa Hemingway: A Personal Memoir*. New York: Random House, Inc., 1966.

Kazin, Alfred. *On Native Grounds*. New York: Renal and Hitchcock, 1942.

Levin, Harry. "Observations on the Style of Ernest Hemingway." *Kenyon Review 13* (Autumn, 1951).

Lewis, Robert W., Jr. *Hemingway on Love*. Austin: University of Texas Press, 1965.

Shaw, Samuel. *Ernest Hemingway*. New York: Frederick Ungar, 1973.

Waldhorn, Arthur. *Ernest Hemingway: A Collection of Criticism*. New York: McGraw Hill, 1973.

Weeks, Robert P. *Hemingway: A Collection of Critical Essays*. Englewood Cliffs, N.J.: Prentice-Hall, 1962.

Young, Philip. *Ernest Hemingway*. New York: Holt, Rinehart and Winston, 1952.

NOTES

NOTES

NOTES